A LIFE LESS
ANXIOUS

A LIFE LESS
ANXIOUS

freedom from panic attacks
and social anxiety without
drugs or therapy

STEVE PAVILANIS

Coauthored by Patricia Alma Lee

ALPEN PUBLISHING COMPANY

CHICAGO • 2010

For information, contact Alpen Publishing Company, 2506 N. Clark St #284, Chicago, IL 60614.

This book does not provide you with official medical advice or an official medical diagnosis. This includes any discussions involving medication. If your physical and/or mental symptoms are causing you great distress or you are experiencing any medical problems, or have any questions about medication, please seek attention from a licensed medical doctor or other such licensed healthcare professional before beginning or altering any treatment plan. In summary, this book is not a substitute for professional healthcare.

This book includes information from many sources, including the author's personal experiences. It is published for general reference and is not intended to be a substitute for independent verification by readers when necessary and appropriate. The publisher and author disclaim any personal liability, directly or indirectly, for advice or information presented within. Although the author and publisher have prepared this manuscript with utmost care and diligence and have made every effort to ensure the accuracy and completeness of the information contained within, we assume no responsibility for errors, inaccuracies, omissions or inconsistencies.

Publisher's Cataloging-in-Publication
(Provided by Quality Books, Inc.)

Pavilanis, Steve.
    A life less anxious : freedom from panic attacks and social anxiety without drugs or therapy / Steve Pavilanis ; coauthored by Patricia Alma Lee.
    p. cm.
    ISBN-13: 978-0-9821401-2-3
    ISBN-10: 0-9821401-2-6

    1. Panic attacks--Treatment--Popular works.
2. Social phobia--Treatment--Popular works. 3. Anxiety--Treatment--Popular works. 4. Self-help techniques.
I. Lee, Patricia A. II. Title.

RC535.P38 2009   616.85'223
                  QBI09-600100

For my mother,
who taught me to see the beauty in life.

ACKNOWLEDGEMENTS

AS A FIRST-TIME AUTHOR and self-publisher, this experience of taking an idea and turning it into a book has been one of the most complicated yet rewarding learning experiences of my life. My sincere thanks to the following people who helped see this labor of love through to completion:

Patricia Alma Lee, my coauthor, developmental editor, and friend, who helped take a rough manuscript full of writing no-nos and polish it into this book.

Graham Van Dixhorn at Write To Your Market, Inc., for helping me find the right words.

Shannon Bodie at Lightbourne, Inc., for her expertise and professionalism in book design and for answering my five million questions.

My friends at Extreme Toastmasters in Chicago, who helped me overcome my fears and provided invaluable feedback for this book.

Very sincere thanks to my family, friends, and loved ones for providing much needed moral support, encouragement, and advice for this book.

Finally, to all who read this book, thank you for your support. May your life be less anxious.

Steve Pavilanis
May 2009

CONTENTS

ABOUT THE AUTHOR

I'M NOT A PSYCHIATRIST, psychologist, medical doctor, or therapist of any sort.

What I am is just a normal guy whose life changed significantly once I experienced my first panic attack. My world was turned completely upside down, and I had never felt so lost in all my life.

I know what it's like to cry yourself to sleep with worry, thinking that you're losing your mind. I know what it's like to lose your freedom and spirit of adventure to a self-imposed and ever-shrinking prison.

I hid from the world at times during a five-year period, ashamed of what I had become. My fears affected every area of my life, robbing me of my outgoing personality and dreams. During this time, I felt as if I was wasting my life.

I spent five years suffering, battling, relapsing, learning about, and eventually conquering my own personal problems with panic and social anxiety. I learned the hard way what really works and what doesn't. I've recorded in this book which tools and techniques can best help you overcome your own personal struggles with anxiety. I also have an idea about who you are. You may be experiencing the same anxiety problems that I did. I felt pain similar to what you are feeling and probably had some of the same fears and scary thoughts as you. But I overcame them and want to show you how you can, too. I authored this book to help you live a more peaceful and fulfilling life. Here's my most important message for you: There is hope.

I've been a social butterfly most of my life. I've had many friends and gotten along with just about everyone. I've often been the guy everyone expects to crack a joke or get up and do something funny. It seems strange for someone with my outgoing personality to develop panic attacks and social anxieties, but it happened to me.

While overcoming my anxiety problems was by far the most difficult thing I have ever done (so far!), it has also been the most rewarding. The ways in which I have grown are beyond measure. Facing my most deep-seated fears forced me to take an honest look at myself and opened my eyes to many wonderful possibilities and insights.

I am very proud of this book. My intention is to share my growth experience and encourage others through it and the related website. I want to help as many people as I can to reclaim their lives.

For further information please visit www.alifelessanxious.com—an online community where you will find helpful anxiety-related resources, and may participate in discussions in our forums.

INTRODUCTION

ANXIETY IS NO FUN. If you've been experiencing severe problems with anxiety in your life, you're not alone. Anxiety disorders are one of the most common mental illnesses in the United States, affecting more than 40 million Americans (National Institute of Mental Health, http://www.nimh.nih.gov/health/publications/anxiety-disorders/introduction.shtml). However, these statistics refer only to those who have sought formal help. Consider that many millions more in the United States alone may never seek treatment due to embarrassment, confusion, or financial constraints.

Today's Western society moves faster than ever. As we become more wired and limited in our social interactions, it's no surprise that scores of us have developed social anxiety problems. In this go-go world, many of us have forgotten (or never learned) how to relax and find peace in our daily lives.

The most frustrating part about anxiety disorders is that there isn't a quick fix. It's not like going to the doctor for a broken arm or nasal infection. No magic pill has been manufactured that will solve your problems. The remedy is much more complex, and that can be frustrating.

Are you ready to get your life back? Do you want to go after the real happiness that you are entitled to? Wouldn't you love to leave the house today and live your life without having your fears determine what you can and cannot do?

The journey is about to begin, and although you may not be sure you are ready, you are. After all, you've taken the first step by picking up this book. I want to let you know that I have poured my heart and soul into every page. I'll share some candid and embarrassing personal stories, ones that I know panic and social anxiety sufferers will understand. Of course, I'll also share some of my triumphs along my personal path to freedom.

You, too, can achieve freedom from your fears. When you do, you will find an inner peace that is the most beautiful, inspiring sensation you could ever imagine. How's that sound?

IT'S NO LONGER TABOO

Anxiety disorders are no longer taboo subjects or viewed as conditions that only happen to "crazy" people. More and more people, including celebrities such as Academy Award-winning actress Nicole Kidman, Today Show weatherman and co-host Willard Scott, Food Network TV star Paula Deen, and NFL star running back Ricky Williams, have come forward to talk about their struggles with panic attacks and social anxiety.

There are also more resources than ever before for panic and anxiety sufferers to access for help. I have read countless books, listened to many audio programs, and even attended therapy sessions to overcome my panic and social anxiety. Fortunately, the help available for treating anxiety disorders is improving.

This book is the culmination of what I've learned along my journey and taken from each experience. From the darkest days that were littered with thoughts of hopelessness and even suicide, to the days I've stood atop the world in triumph, it's all recorded here.

This is my way of giving something back. I truly believe anxiety came into my life for a reason. My suffering made me face things about myself that I had continually avoided. Now I feel a sense of enlightenment and peace, which may have not occurred otherwise.

This book is divided into three parts. In Part 1, I tell you my own personal story of how panic attacks and social anxiety suddenly appeared in my life, and my initial efforts to find answers and seek relief.

In Part 2, you can learn from the many lessons I struggled with in my search for a cure for my anxiety problems. Why did I have so many relapses? Breathing and relaxation techniques that work are given, and the benefits of meditation and how to do it are explained.

Additionally, the faulty thinking patterns of anxiety sufferers and how to break free from them are explained. This section also includes a detailed plan for how to systematically face and defeat your fears.

Part 3 is a summary of how to apply all of the lessons and techniques described in Part 2. You will learn through step-by-step examples about the situations I feared, how I conquered them, how you can prevent relapsing into anxiety, and the lifestyle changes you can make to encourage a peaceful and fulfilling life.

I hope this book reaches deep into your heart and awakens that zest and excitement for an enlightened life that is begging to come out of you.

Five years after I experienced the first of many panic attacks, they have been defeated. I won't have one again, and I want you to have that feeling as well. Don't you?

Admittedly, I took a long and painful road. But now that a roadmap has been drawn, you can find your way much faster to a healthier, happier life.

Please believe that there is hope for you. It doesn't matter how desperate you are. Hope is always there. The power to change your life resides within you at this very moment. I'm going to help you find it and unleash it!

> *"Deep within man dwell those slumbering powers; powers that would astonish him, that he never dreamed of possessing; forces that would revolutionize his life if aroused and put into action."*
>
> ORISON SWETT MARDEN
> (Founder of *Success* magazine and motivational author)

PART I

A LIFE CHANGER: MY FIRST PANIC ATTACK

A LIFE CHANGER:
MY FIRST PANIC ATTACK

THE FOURTH OF JULY HOLIDAY when I was twenty-five years old will forever be etched into my memory. I wish I could tell you this was the day I hit a home run while playing third base for the Chicago Cubs or won a stage in the Tour de France, but it wasn't. This day, my first panic attack happened.

At the time, I had been living and working in Germany for a little more than a year and had become quite comfortable living abroad. I was learning the language and had established a solid group of good friends with whom I often traveled. During that holiday week of the Fourth of July, my best friend, Robbie, came to Europe for a visit. I took a few days off work to meet up and travel with him.

On July 3, we did our best to drink all of the beer in the city of Prague in the Czech Republic. Judging by our brutal hangovers the next day, we must have come close. Exhausted, cranky, and severely dehydrated, we hit the road bound for the Bavarian Alps in southern Germany.

We drove for countless hours through uneventful farmland while crammed into a comically small European car with no air conditioning. The misery was amplified due to our pathetic physical states. We made frequent stops for caffeine that kept us awake but dehydrated us even further. Eventually, around nightfall, we had gone as far as we could go given our condition. We found a small family-owned hotel in the middle of nowhere in Bavaria and settled in for the night.

With peaceful mountains and a clear, babbling brook for a backdrop, our exhausted bodies couldn't have been in a better place to sleep and recharge. But that didn't happen. Instead, that night I had the strangest experience.

Except for the tranquil sound of the stream just outside the window, it was very quiet. However, as I lay in bed trying to fall asleep, I noticed my heart was starting to beat rapidly. The more I became aware of it, the faster it beat. The harder I tried to ignore it, the more I couldn't!

After a few minutes, I bolted to my feet, scared. I thought, "Am I having a heart attack?" My commotion awoke Robbie, who seemed quite startled. This freaked me out even more. I told him that I couldn't catch my breath, and that my heart was beating out of control.

He said to just calm down, that it was simply a panic attack, and he had even had one once. Although you'd think it would, his explanation didn't help me. I felt completely lost and out of control.

I remember doing everything I could to try to slow my heartbeat. I went outside into the fresh, chilly mountain air and paced around. I tried to wear myself out physically by doing push-ups. I ran in place. I ran short sprints. I did jumping jacks. I tried to breathe deeply, but nothing worked!

After about thirty minutes of absolute hell, my body and my emotions finally calmed down. My heartbeat returned to normal, but I felt like it could resume pounding furiously at any second. This feeling of being on the edge lasted for hours, which really took a toll on me. With my nerves frayed and my confidence shaken, I lay in bed trying to take my mind off scary thoughts. Somehow I eventually fell asleep or, more accurately, passed out from exhaustion.

The next day I awoke fatigued and still on edge. I was afraid to have any caffeine that morning, so I skipped the coffee. Robbie realized how bad I must have felt to refuse a cup of fresh European coffee. He knows how much I love the stuff.

I felt as if I could spiral into another panic attack at any moment, but I did my best to hide this. After one more day of sightseeing in the Alps, we drove to Munich where I dropped Robbie off. I then raced straight to the emergency room at the hospital in town.

Trying to explain to the hospital receptionist what was happening to me in German (mind you, I was only about 30% fluent at the time) when I didn't even know how to explain it in English was a train wreck. Luckily, the doctors spoke fluent English and I was able to convey what my problems and symptoms were.

"You just need to relax," said the doctor.

"Okay, that sounds great, doc. *How* do I relax? I feel like I'm losing my mind here. I feel weird and spacey, like I'm not in my own body. Everything feels surreal."

Sadly he didn't have an answer for me. I couldn't relax. I didn't know how. It was like telling a rabid pit bull on cocaine to stop gnawing off your leg!

The doctor took mercy on me and gave me some Valium. The side effects made me feel numb and tired. The scary feelings and thoughts were still there, but they weren't as severe. The next day I returned to my apartment in Frankfurt. The first action I took was to start making appointments to have myself checked out.

Because I have a scientific engineering background, I took the logical approach. Clearly something was very wrong, something in my head. Perhaps a tumor, maybe a blood clot—*something* must have been causing this.

I put myself through just about every physical test modern medicine offers—blood work, CAT scans, even some weird electro-nerve tests the German doctors recommended. To my great surprise, they found I was in good health. I wanted so badly for the doctors to say they had found something physical and tangible that could be fixed. Instead, they recommended I see a psychiatrist and think about taking medication.

Learning that my problem was psychological in nature was devastating. I felt lost, confused, and scared. I vividly remember sitting in a doctor's office in Frankfurt, waiting for yet another test. All I kept thinking was *what a waste*. Twenty-five years old, reasonably intelligent, outgoing, and with my whole life ahead of me—and I'm losing my mind. All my dreams for my life would have to be cancelled. I began to sink into a deep depression.

To think that I legitimately *needed* to see a psychiatrist depressed me further. Still, I was hoping that it could help. The only doctor I could get my insurance to pay for was Russian and hadn't spoken English in twenty years. She insisted, however (in German), that she could understand most of what I told her in English. Thus my therapy sessions were a mix of broken German and first-grade-level English.

When she didn't seem to understand what I was saying in English, I'd try saying it in German. I wasn't sure whether I was telling her about my anxiety or the schnitzel I had for lunch! Anyone listening to the conversation would have probably jumped out the window in frustration. This attempt at therapy wasn't helping.

Having reached my mid-twenties without having anything too serious besides a few minor bouts of depression in high school (come on, who isn't depressed in high school?), I figured I had beaten the odds and escaped unscathed by mental illness. But now it seemed I just reached into the bag of mental issues later in life and found my fun in the form of panic disorder and social anxiety.

MY MEDICATION EXPERIENCE

My psychiatrist eventually prescribed a selective serotonin reuptake inhibitor (SSRI). As defined by WebMD.com, "(SSRIs) are a newer form of antidepressant. These drugs work by altering the amount of a chemical in the brain called serotonin." (http://www. webmd.com/depression/medication-options). She told me some of her patients had found it helpful. I was very skeptical that it would help, but I prayed that it would.

Taking prescription psychoactive drugs for the first time felt surreal. I knew they would be altering my brain chemistry, and this terrified me. I already felt as if I had no control of my mind and thoughts, so how would I even know if the medication was working? Could it make my thoughts even scarier, or would I somehow magically be my old self again?

In a few days, I began to feel the effects of the medication. I was a walking zombie. I felt as if my life was playing out in slow motion, as if there was a dense cloud set atop my brain. Some friends mentioned that my quick wit was gone, that I seemed "off." My sense of adventure and spontaneity had disappeared, too. But this wasn't the worst of it.

Some of these drugs have other significant side effects people don't want to talk about. A doctor would call it "erectile dysfunction." As a virile twenty-five-year-old single man, I refer to it as one of the worst experiences imaginable.

For the first time in my life, my libido almost died. My erections were very infrequent, and when I did have sex, I felt so mentally and physically numb that climaxing was nearly impossible.

Sex had constantly been on my mind since puberty. Suddenly, this was gone.

As devastated as I was, imagine me explaining these side effects to the women I dated during this time: "It's not you, it's me... seriously!"

None of them seemed to grasp how desperately I felt I needed the medication. I couldn't stop taking it, despite these embarrassing situations. I asked a doctor for help, and he prescribed Viagra. You'd think giving a healthy young man such a drug would turn him into a walking erection. Yet it still wasn't enough to offset the effects of the anxiety medication and allow me to function normally.

While at work, I was very aware of my scary thoughts. The medication helped, but I still didn't know if I really was okay. I tried to maintain a low profile. I desperately hoped no one would discover this horrible truth about me—that I was no longer in control of myself. Although I thought I appeared calm, inside I was living a nightmare.

Unhappy with the side effects and lack of profound improvement with the first few medications, I went back to the doctor. I was willing to try anything that would stop the panic attacks. I was a frantic, anxious mess. If the doctor had recommended that I smoke crack and run naked around the city, I would have. In total, I tried five or six different anti-anxiety/antidepressant medications.

I distinctly remember one drug causing a powerful spacey feeling, while another one caused a sharp pain in my head as if I was being stabbed with a Samurai sword. Imagine how awful this was for a confused and panic-stricken person to experience. It was like throwing napalm into my campfire of anxiety and worry.

By now, I felt I was probably insane, but *how* insane was the question. Were the drugs keeping me from losing it or causing me to lose it? Did anybody else see that pink elephant over there?

Some medications made me nauseous. Some made me sleep almost twenty-four hours a day. I remember taking a weeklong trip to Barcelona, Spain, with a girlfriend one summer. Despite being completely sedated from medication, I still had a mild panic attack on the plane just before takeoff. I somehow gathered myself and calmed down near the end of the flight. That may be attributed to the two double bourbons I ordered.

Driving the rental car from the airport and into Barcelona, I was exhausted. The espresso I had gulped down near baggage claim after arriving had done nothing to snap me out of my daze. We pulled into a roadside café where I had a double espresso and ordered another one for the road.

I felt like a complete disaster. The injections of caffeine I pumped into my system were wreaking havoc on my body, while the antidepressants I was on still gripped my mind. I strove to have fun on the trip, and for a few beautiful moments I did enjoy it. Still, I could feel how out of whack my entire system was. Pouring vast amounts of anxiety medication, caffeine, and alcohol into my body every day was not good. Go figure! I wondered what was going to come first, an ulcer, heart attack, or kidney failure.

Self-medication is popular. Many people in our society are resorting to it to relieve their suffering. We turn into drug addicts and drunks trying to find a happier place. As for me, I couldn't sleep. I was terrified of going to bed, for I would lie there and have to face my thoughts. Remember, lying in bed one night while trying to fall asleep was the setting in which I had my first panic attack. I found television a much-needed distraction, often falling asleep watching reruns of *The Simpsons*.

I felt as if I needed something to sedate me. I was living in Germany, where drinking good beer is a way of life. I'd found a solution! For months, I had more than a few every night (alone) to knock myself out. It worked. For a good six months, I lived my life in a daze.

Before my first panic attack, I didn't understand how people could let themselves become addicted to drugs or alcohol to the point where they would abuse while by themselves. Now I understood. I felt humbled and vulnerable knowing I had become one of those people who felt he had to drink to feel normal. I had thought previously I was too strong and determined to ever become like that.

Why do people self-medicate? For me, it was an escape. Alcohol allowed me to live in the moment briefly every evening and forget my troubles.

Alcohol is a depressant, however, and while I gained a small sliver of what I interpreted as freedom every night while I was drunk, I was sinking deeper and deeper into depression.

As autumn arrived, I remained on various medications and my world continued to shrink. I had lost the desire to explore and try new and unfamiliar things. Despite living in the heart of Europe, I didn't travel much. I was having enough trouble trying to be comfortable in my own apartment and at work. This transformation depressed me further, because before the panic attacks, I had lived to travel and experience the unknown.

I became more and more closed off to the world. Fearful a panic attack would occur at any time, I avoided any setting in which I wouldn't have control and be able to escape if needed. If you stop and think about all the situations that includes, maybe you can imagine the shell of a life that remains. I spent most of my time alone on my couch.

I no longer went to the grocery store after work, because what if I had a panic attack while waiting in a long line? I couldn't just throw down my groceries and run away—I would be stuck in the skinny lane between registers with a cart full of groceries! So, I shopped only just before the stores closed. I missed out on the great fresh bread and meat available from the German bakeries and butchers. Sadly, this no longer mattered to me; for in my eyes I didn't deserve the good things in life. I barely felt alive.

I absolutely dreaded riding the train to work, but given my geographic location, I had no alternative. Often, I would go to work very early to avoid the main rush hour, and stay late at work to avoid it afterwards. Fears of losing control haunted my mind when I was on public transportation. Just as bad was the nervous anticipation before each trip.

Meetings at work became a nightmare. Scary thoughts plagued my mind, and all I could think of were the most awful scenarios. What if I had to run out of an important meeting while my boss was talking? What if I just stood up and screamed obscenities during a keynote speech at an all-hands meeting? What if I picked up a chair and for no reason threw it through a window? I would often develop cold sweats in meetings trying to suppress these scary thoughts. Naturally, avoidance set in. I often called in sick to work on days when I knew there was a big meeting or seminar I would have to attend.

"Fear kills more people than death. Death kills us but once, and we usually don't even know it. But fear kills us over and over again. Suddenly at times, and brutally at other times."

GENERAL GEORGE S. PATTON
(famous and often-quoted U.S. Army general during World War II)

By that Christmas, I was still on a solid regimen of anxiety medication and alcohol. My only goal was to keep myself from losing my mind—although I often wondered if I had already lost that battle. It's impossible to put into words how upsetting it was to me to think that, at twenty-five years old, my best years had already passed. I felt as if I had already peaked and was now stuck in a downward spiral straight to hell.

I had been with my girlfriend at the time for about six months. While our relationship had started out very well, it was suffering due to my anxiety problems. Still, we made plans to visit both of our families in the United States during Christmas. I was quite anxious about meeting her family and about introducing her to mine.

Despite her warm and welcoming family, I had several panic attacks during my visit. The most notable occurred at a dinner with her family, not that it was a stiff or awkward situation, for they were all very friendly. I was just a wreck, plain and simple. The usual dreaded what-if thoughts plagued my mind, and I couldn't enjoy the wonderful food. Instead I slurped down enough wine to help me ignore my scary thoughts.

As the months went by and spring arrived, I started to feel better. Maybe my mindset was aided by the improving weather, who knows? I still had the negative side effects from the medication, but I hadn't had a full-blown panic attack in more than two months. I started to think that no longer having a properly functioning penis, a quick sense of wit or a zest for living might be worth it! I almost thought my panic attacks might be gone for good, and I felt much more confident. However, one fateful spring day changed that.

ROLLER COASTER RIDE

Along with a friend, I signed up for a one-day training course away from the office. What happened that morning haunted me for years.

The training class was the usual cold, stiff, and formal German office. I never had been very comfortable in this setting. The attendees were dressed impeccably with not a hair out of place. They looked very intelligent and accomplished, spoke multiple languages fluently, and seemed extremely professional. Since my self-esteem had taken a nosedive over the previous twelve months, it was an intimidating scene.

As in most classroom settings, the instructor asked us to introduce ourselves to the group. This should have been no big deal for me. I've been introducing myself to classes since I was in kindergarten. As the introductions started on the other side of the room, however, I began to feel very anxious as I anticipated speaking to the group.

At first, it was just the usual butterflies and jump in heartbeat. But suddenly, something else happened. Some of my horrible what-if thoughts gained momentum. Then there was a crack in the dam of my mind. At first just a trickle, then the entire river of horrible thoughts broke through and flooded my mind.

My heartbeat raced off the charts. I looked down and could see the top button of my neatly pressed shirt tremble with every mighty pulse. I couldn't breathe. I couldn't swallow. I couldn't run out of the classroom before it was my turn—that would be too obvious. What if I couldn't talk when they got to me? What if they could hear how ridiculously nervous I was? What if I just passed out in front of them? What was I going to do?

I was in a full-blown panic attack—one of my worst. When it finally was my turn, I didn't know what to do. I didn't think I could even force words to come out of my mouth. Would there be any sound at all? Would my voice crack like it did when I was going through puberty, embarrassing me in front of everyone? My heart was beating so fast I wasn't sure it was even physically possible to talk and hear my voice over my heartbeat.

I signaled that I needed a moment and tried to sip some water from a glass. My hand was shaking so wildly, I am sure those close to me noticed. I used the cover of needing a drink to mask my trembling voice and acted as if I just had a tickle in my throat and couldn't speak. I took a quick sip from the glass and, with a mouth half full of water, I attempted to speak. Somehow words actually did come out, which was a surprise. My voice shook at first but became normal by the end of my three-sentence introduction.

When the introductions were finished, I was still on edge, but no longer panicking. My heart was still pounding, just not to the point where I felt like it might explode. I had survived, which gave me some relief. However, I was paralyzed with the fear that I would be asked to speak in front of the group again.

I was dumbfounded. What the hell was that? I hadn't had a panic attack like that in months. I wasn't stuck in a crowded elevator or train. All I had had to do was say three sentences about myself in front of twenty colleagues. That was it. So what had triggered my panic attack?

Afterwards, I was absolutely fried and exhausted, both mentally and physically. The rest of the class went by, but I don't remember much of it. I was in a daze. Luckily, I didn't have to speak again, which was all that I cared about. Boarding the train home that night, I felt broken and confused.

Just when I thought I had made progress and gotten beyond my panic attacks, they had reappeared with a vengeance. The weird part was how and when they had decided to reappear, while waiting to introduce myself to a classroom of colleagues. Why?

I realized then and there that the anxiety medication was only doing one thing... numbing me. Numbing my mind, numbing my body, and clearly not fixing the real problem, whatever that was. Obviously there was still something deeply wrong with me, but what?

After some deep reflection, I realized that none of the six medications I had tried had eliminated my panic attacks. I had gained a false sense of security while on the last medication, which was destroyed by this one panic attack. I decided to quit all anxiety medication cold turkey.

Whatever my problem was, I now believed that it couldn't be fixed by medication. I had tried the most successful and popular medications, and I was still suffering. I felt I was losing my mind either way, so I might as well get off the medication and get my personality back. Hey, at least my penis would work again!

With my relationship with my live-in girlfriend ruined and a job I had lost interest in doing, I had to change my life. The two years I had committed to live and work in Europe had almost expired, and I began to mentally prepare to return to the United States.

With wheels in motion for my return, I was sad to leave the many wonderful (pre-panic problems) experiences of Europe behind. However, I knew my best chance at a fresh start would be in a familiar American setting. Not only would I be able to watch baseball and college football games again, I could finally tell an American psychiatrist in plain English that I was losing my mind!

A FRESH START IN THE WINDY CITY

Chicago: An exciting new city, new career opportunities, and the potential for new friends. Despite my excitement, seeds of doubt and uncertainty were still planted deep within my mind. My stance was to ignore them as long as possible. I hoped that my change of scenery would help.

I distinctly remember being on the phone with a Chicago office representative and accepting the offer while still in Germany. I felt happy, but that was short-lived. I knew that I would once again have to face my nightmare office scenarios.

I thought, "I may seem successful and smart, but if and when people find out about my panic attacks and fear of public speaking, I'll be exposed. What will they think if they know the *real* me?" After taking care of a billion details, I moved to Chicago and fell in love with the city. I quickly made some new friends and had exactly zero boring weekends that first summer. However, no amount of fun could make me forget about the fears and anxieties I was doing my best to suppress.

A fateful commute

Chicago's elevated train mass transit system (referred to as "the el") is a well-known landmark. The tracks twist and turn between skyscrapers downtown and inches away from buildings in the different neighborhoods. It provides a cool and unique way to see this massive and beautiful city.

To get to work, I had to catch the el near my apartment. I had to climb up 25 feet of stairs to get to the boarding platform. Late one particular morning, I frantically raced up the stairs to catch a departing train. I crammed inside the car and the loudspeaker sang its usual "*Ding dong*, doors closing."

Still catching my breath, my heart continued to beat quickly. The train was very crowded. I was shoulder to shoulder with fellow passengers, and we filled the standing room area. I had been riding crowded trains for two years in Germany, so none of this was unfamiliar to me.

The el train moves very slowly at times, sometimes taking up to ten minutes between stops. As I stood there in the crowded and barely moving train, I suddenly noticed that my heart hadn't slowed down. Out of nowhere, I could feel the dread and panic beginning to fill my mind. "What if I can't slow my heart beat down? Oh, God! Not again!" My symptoms grew worse. My breathing became rapid and shallow, my heart pounded and my legs turned to jelly. I had a panic attack. Again!?

I tried to take my mind off the fact that I was having a breakdown in front of an entire trainload of people. Seconds were hours. I prayed under my breath. I opened my workbag, searching for a distraction. With my heart pounding through my chest, the el finally pulled up to the next stop.

I assumed everyone in the train car was aware that I was extremely anxious. I wanted to get out, but then again, if I got out after one stop, wouldn't that arouse more suspicion? Wouldn't it be obvious that I was terrified and having a panic attack and was a total weirdo who didn't belong there?

As the doors slid open, even more people crammed in. I could barely move an arm, we were so tightly packed. The loudspeaker rang once again, triggering a reaction. I bolted out the door and onto the platform. The doors closed and the train sped away. In a few minutes, I calmed down, but my legs were weak and my entire body was trembling. I felt worthless and rejected. What a coward I had been! I was so upset that I called in sick to work from my cell phone right there on the platform.

I could have walked home, but instead I actually went to the other side of the platform to catch the same train in the opposite direction toward my apartment. I knew that the train headed away from downtown would be nearly empty and caught the first one. I was a bit nervous climbing aboard, but it soon passed and before I knew it I had gone one stop and was back where I had started.

This panic attack left a deep scar on me. More than a year passed before I even dared to ride the el again.

"I'd like to thank the Academy"

During all of this, I'm pretty sure that none of my friends suspected I was suffering so intensely. Hell! I've had panic attacks in front of most of them, and I doubt they had any idea. My façade was first-rate. I appeared to be in good spirits, while inside I was dying a thousand deaths. I deserved an award for my acting.

I had shared my experiences of panic attacks and anxiety with only a couple doctors. Eventually I became so petrified of having to speak in weekly status meetings that I pulled my boss aside and told him what I was going through. I explained that I was having problems with anxiety, and, if I ever acted weird in a meeting, please let it pass. I emphasized that I cared about my job and wanted to do well, but I sometimes just couldn't seem to control my anxieties and fears.

He was sympathetic and helpful, and something very humanizing happened. He revealed that he too had many social anxiety issues. He even asked me for some advice! Advice from me!? I don't know—hmmm... drink too much and hide from your fears, hoping they magically go away? Seriously though, I told him what little I knew and gave him the names of some doctors.

I felt some relief. I no longer had to hide my anxiety problems from my boss. Still, every day in the office remained a struggle.

As my condition worsened, I began to search for help on the Internet. I was hoping to find a support group or specialized therapy program for anxiety problems. When I saw that there was an anxiety counseling center in Chicago, I decided to research it. I went into an empty conference room during a quiet afternoon at work and dialed the phone number three or four times before I had the courage to type in the seventh and final digit. Talk about a guy who needed help! I could barely bring myself to call the place that might be able to help me.

I talked with the director of the center. He seemed calm and welcoming, and so I placed my name on the waiting list for the next group. I was eager to get started with a group, yet at the same time I was completely terrified of having to speak at a meeting.

Another thought I had was *what if this didn't work?* What if I finally got to this anxiety treatment center, and I'm hands down the worst case they've ever seen? What if they say that I'm too far gone and can't be saved? I mean, if this place couldn't help me, nobody could, right?

Finally, the group was set up and the meetings were scheduled for every Saturday morning. The first morning arrived, and as I boarded the bus to the session, my nerves were frayed. I couldn't eat breakfast and I skipped my usual morning coffee. I understood by now that caffeine would only compound my anxiety.

Once I arrived, I paced around the building's lobby for ten minutes even though I knew where to go, delaying the inevitable. As I made my way up the elevator and located the office, I noticed how wildly my hand was shaking as I reached for the doorknob. "Wow," I thought, "this is going to suck!"

I opened the door and saw fifteen chairs with only a few people seated. I felt dread that all the chairs would soon be filled with people to whom I would have to introduce myself. Would I flip out and have to run out of the room? The space was small and cramped, which only fed my worry.

The room did fill, and some of us exchanged informal hellos, but remember: these were anxiety sufferers. I'm sure *everyone* in that room was feeling just as anxious as I was, although no one seemed to show it. For the first few minutes I sat there, I felt that at any moment I might have to bolt out of the room and escape.

The session was run well. I thanked God that I didn't have to say a single word. The instructor was calming and simply talked about what brought us there. As relaxed as he was, I was perched on the edge of my seat the entire session. Miraculously, I made it through the meeting. I hadn't spoken or actively contributed to the meeting, but the mere fact that I didn't run was a huge victory for me.

Walking out of the session and then around downtown afterwards, I couldn't stop grinning. What was this strange and unfamiliar feeling? It was budding self-confidence and a positive feeling of self-worth. I had almost forgotten what they felt like.

Ever since my panic attack on the el, even riding the bus caused me tremendous anxiety. However, as I boarded it for the ride home that morning, I clearly remember I had no anxiety. Somehow, conquering my fear of attending the meeting that morning had diminished my fear of riding the bus.

> *"You cannot discover new oceans unless you have the courage to lose sight of the shore."*
>
> ANDRE GIDE
> (French author and winner of the Nobel Prize in literature in 1947)

During that winter, I attended the group anxiety sessions nearly every Saturday. I won't lie. I occasionally skipped sessions when I was feeling particularly anxious, but most of the time I went despite being afraid.

We spent the first two months learning specifics about panic and anxiety. I gained a better understanding of what my body was doing when I had panic attacks and why. I still, however, had to overcome them. Eventually we began the most vital phase of the healing process—facing our fears.

Two situations had caused my worst panic attacks—riding the crowded el train and speaking to a group of people in an office meeting. These were the fears I needed to face.

Just the thought of facing either was enough to deeply upset me. Every Saturday morning, I was encouraged to tell the group about my previous week and any noteworthy anxiety I had experienced. Because my fears of public speaking were so strong, this weekly update terrified me. However, by simply attending the meetings every week and speaking briefly, I was facing my public speaking fears. Each week was a small victory that boosted my self-confidence.

While I was slowly but surely facing my fear of public speaking, I was still petrified of crowded public transportation. I was riding the least-full buses to and from work, but I knew it was time to start pushing myself beyond my comfort zone in this area as well.

> *"Be not afraid of growing slowly;*
> *be afraid only of standing still."*
> CHINESE PROVERB

So, I started small. Instead of letting the mostly full buses go by while I waited for an empty one, I began to board the first bus that came by. As the weeks passed, I pushed myself further and further. Some days I just didn't feel up to it, however, and then I would wait for an emptier bus. I viewed this as okay, as progress often entails taking two steps forward, one step back. The most important point was that I didn't give up.

Over time, my fear of crowded buses diminished. Sure, I was still anxious before boarding, but it became easier as the weeks and then months went by.

While I had made great progress on conquering my fear of crowded buses, I hadn't set foot in the el for almost a year. I had to create a plan of attack, but first let me emphasize just how terrified I was of riding it again.

"*Ding dong*, doors closing." Even if you're not on the platform for the el, you can hear this announcement a block away. I was so frightened of the el that if I walked near a station and heard the loudspeakers, my stomach would churn with fear. I had some serious work ahead of me to overcome this.

Knowing the el was busiest at rush hours in the morning and evening, I decided to ride it during my lunch hour. None of my co-workers or friends would know.

After a weekend of dreading it, Monday came and my stomach was a complete mess. Although I felt like I had eaten my bodyweight in tacos from a Tijuana street vendor, it was just stress. When lunchtime arrived, I buttoned up my coat with trembling hands and headed for the elevators.

Walking to the el stop, I was nauseous with fear. I would have rather been on my way to fight Mike Tyson. Getting badly beaten and having my ear bitten off sounded easier than this. Couldn't a car or bus hit me along the way, please?

At the station, I climbed up the stairs to the platform. My heart was already pounding, and exerting myself while climbing the stairs actually provided some relief.

On the platform, I peered down the tracks but there wasn't a train in sight. I would have to stand there and mentally stew over my impending train ride, which made my anxiety levels soar.

I had planned on riding the train just one stop. That seems easy enough, right? Let me explain something else to you about the el. It sometimes breaks down and stops while en route. You never know when you're going to hear the loudspeakers, *"Beep beep beep—*May we have your attention please. We are experiencing a delay waiting for signals up ahead. We will begin moving shortly and appreciate your patience." Such a delay can last anywhere from a minute or two to ten. While it hasn't happened to me, some of my friends have told me they've been stuck in the el for more than an hour.

After nervously pacing around the platform, the first Brown Line train finally approached. I walked to the end of the platform to get into the last car, usually the least crowded. With my heart pounding and my stomach in my throat, I stepped inside. I was too wound up to sit down, so I stood near the doors. Psychologically it was easier for me to stand there, as that was the only way out of the train.

"Ding dong, doors closing," came the announcement I hadn't heard from inside the el in almost a year. This was it—I was stuck, I was committed. As the train began to move, I was incredibly anxious but not panicking. If a panic attack is rated from 1 (cool and calm) to 100 (freaking out), I was at about 85. I felt as though I could lose my composure and start trying to pry the doors open at any second, but I was doing my best to focus on my breathing and get through it. As we approached the turn before the next station, the train slowed down almost to a stop, which is normal. For me however, this was slow torture. My anxieties were rising,

but before I knew it, the turn was complete and we were at the next stop.

By now, I had calmed down a bit. Not reacting and fighting through it helped. The doors opened at the first stop, but I didn't step outside. I decided to be brave and stay aboard for one more stop.

The second stop was very close and required no turns, so before I knew it, we had arrived. The third stop, however, would require the train to take turn that involved passing a track switch for all trains entering and exiting the downtown loop. Translation: trains often have to sit and wait for other trains to go through the switch. This was not yet something I wanted to experience, so I quit while I was ahead. I got out at the second stop.

I stepped onto the platform in triumph! I had just accomplished something that I had built up in my mind over the past year as impossible. It was only a small step, but I had gotten through it. I had set the wheels of recovery in motion.

As the weeks went by, I continued making progress. Each day over my lunch break, I pushed myself to ride the el and face my fears. After a few weeks, I was riding it almost all the way around the downtown loop.

The months went by, and eventually I reached the point where I could ride the el again even during the crowded rush hour. I had small relapses here and there, but I stayed determined.

WHAT GOES UP. . .

Crowded elevators were another fear of mine, so one day I felt I was ready to really push the envelope. I just happened to work a block away from the tallest building in the United States, the Sears Tower. I decided I would use my lunch hour, as I had in conquering my fear of the el, to face this fear.

Anticipating facing a difficult situation was like torture. I agonized and imagined the worst-case scenarios over and over in my mind. If I was going to do something difficult, I just wanted to get it over with as soon as possible.

Going to the top of the Sears Tower isn't as simple as catching an elevator and riding up. You are led into a theater with more than twenty other people and shown a short film about the history of the building. The anxiety I felt while seated there was tremendous.

When the film ended, it was go-time. We walked through the narrow hallway to the elevators, led like cattle to slaughter. As with any tall building observatory tour, they pack people into the elevator.

I was one of the last ones to be let in. Seeing an excited little kid eager to enjoy the elevator ride helped take some edge off. When the doors closed and we started up, my anxiety dropped almost immediately. I started to smile, knowing I had this thing beat.

Thus, the three-minute ride to the top was sheer bliss. As the elevator doors opened, the entire observation level was filled with sunshine. I felt a deep soul-warming feeling throughout my entire body. It was complete elation, the highest of highs.

I walked around the floor taking in the views, completely at peace. It's funny, the strange looks you get when you walk around with a huge smile on your face, but who cares! I was smiling my ass off because I was deeply happy for the first time in a long time. Tears welled in my eyes as I stared off into the distance from the 110th floor.

After five months of attending the weekly therapy sessions, my anxiety class ended. We had started with more than a dozen attendees, but only a handful completed the course. We congratulated one another and received certificates of achievement from our instructor. We knew we had certainly made tremendous progress.

While I felt I had come very close to conquering my fears of crowded public transportation, I still had fears about public speaking. Our instructor told me I was welcome to come back and speak to the next group to share my story.

I took him up on the offer a few times over the following months. Each time it became easier. I found sharing my story therapeutic. I felt a sincere connection with everyone in the room, and I hoped the stories of some of my successes could help to inspire them in their own struggles. I was baring it all, coming clean about my fears and worries, and it was incredibly liberating.

I had been guest speaking at the anxiety sessions for other groups, but I still avoided doing what I knew I needed to do—attend Toastmasters.

You may have already heard of Toastmasters, a large international, nonprofit organization with hundreds of chapters worldwide. Each chapter meets every week or two to offer a supportive environment in which to practice and improve public speaking.

Given my paralyzing fear of public speaking, I knew it was exactly what I needed.

Unfortunately, I chickened out. For whatever reasons, I still didn't think I was ready for Toastmasters. I told myself I had done enough.

AM I WELL NOW?

The next summer was a good one. I was back riding public transportation and taking crowded cabs with my friends without even thinking twice about it. I had gained a bit more responsibility at work and had to speak more on our daily conference calls, which was proving to be a good challenge. Still, I didn't feel I had come close to conquering my public-speaking fears and was ever fearful of being put on the spot and being "found out."

I had done such a good job on a project at work that my boss wanted me to present the results to a dozen colleagues. Uh-oh. My ultimate fear became reality. It was now time to pay the price for not facing my public-speaking fears. I acted happy and eager on the outside, but inside I knew I'd end up pulling the freakin' fire alarm, if that's what it took to get out of giving this presentation.

I simply didn't see any plausible way in which I could actually pull this off. The very thought of introducing myself to a group of people in a meeting terrified me. And here I was being asked to make an hour-long presentation on the work my team had done. No way José! I promised myself I would find a way out.

I took the coward's way out and went home "sick" hours before the meeting. Luckily for me, my boss didn't press the issue and didn't ask me to present at a later date. I was face to face with my fear, and like so many times in the past, I ran.

Early that summer, I became a free man. Not free from my anxiety but from the daily grind of the office. I was working as a consultant for a large firm, and my project with a banking client was abruptly terminated following a company merger. This happens sometimes, and as a consultant I would be assigned a new project. I was supposed to help seek a new assignment, but I didn't. I wanted to hold out for a position with the same client once the merger was completed.

That summer I truly experienced Chicago. I got back in shape, explored the city daily on my bicycle, and relaxed. At some point, I would have to face my worst fear—getting back to work. Then I would have to introduce myself to yet another group of co-workers.

Something else happened. I was losing my confidence in riding crowded public transportation, because I rarely took it any more. I no longer was forced to endure the crowds at rush hour, because I had no office to report to. So I didn't. I didn't voluntarily place myself in challenging situations and quickly fell back into old, unhealthy patterns. I could feel all the progress I had made with my anxiety slowly slipping away.

Near the end of the summer, I was assigned to oversee a nine-person team at the same client. While I was glad that I had a paycheck, the prospect of being in charge of nine people was daunting. Not because I was afraid of the work itself. No. That wasn't the problem. I knew I could do a good job. I was terrified of the amount of public speaking in large meetings this role would certainly entail. I accepted the new role despite my concerns and had two weeks to sweat and worry about my return to the office. During this time, I floated my résumé around to see what else was out there. I received a few bites of interest, but one that really grabbed my attention involved returning to work in Germany.

I took the job in Germany, which meant I'd be working for a firm based in Kansas City. I received a huge pay raise and a chance for a new start in my career, something that made me very happy.

The plan called for me to fly to Kansas City every week where I would learn the firm's software and receive training for a couple months before heading to Germany to work at the client site. I was happy for the change of professional scenery and eager to work for what seemed to be a fun and young startup firm.

Before my first trip to Kansas City, however, I was a nervous wreck. I would have to introduce myself to this new group of people at a company meeting. The firm was full of very accomplished, well-educated and well-rounded go-getters who in my mind were just about perfect. I couldn't sleep for days before my first flight to the new office. I kept replaying the worst-case scenarios over and over in my mind.

Lying on the couch the night before my first flight, I was restless. My heart raced over and over again in waves. I became so distraught, I'd have to walk around my apartment, trying to get my mind off of what I anticipated. Finally, I started cracking beers to numb myself and quiet my mind. I doubt I got two hours of sleep that night.

The flight in the morning was half-full, allowing me room to stretch out and try to relax. Afterward, I picked up a rental car at the airport and distinctly remember how spacey and out of body I felt while driving from the airport to the office. I wanted that drive to last forever. I wanted the car to break down on the side of the road. Part of me wanted to yank the wheel and crash the car into an embankment to avoid having to go to the office.

As usual, the trip went about a billion times better than I thought it would. While I became more at ease, the toll was heavy on my body from all of my anticipatory anxiety. I suffered from an upset stomach and even had a lovely gigantic cold sore appear on my upper lip that lasted for about a month. Oh, how I love meeting new people with one of those on my face!

After getting settled with the new company for a little more than a month, it was time for my return to the land of beer, chocolate, and lederhosen. I was extremely excited to revisit a place I loved so much, but also tremendously anxious at the prospect of facing more stiff German meetings.

The flight to Germany left around 7:30 p.m. and put us in Frankfurt around 9:00 a.m. I usually don't sleep much on flights, and given my anxiety over the upcoming meetings the next day, this flight was no exception. I did, however, enjoy the free booze that international flights allot, as it helped me doze off. But as the plane filled with daylight from the rising sun over Europe, I found myself absolutely exhausted and dehydrated. The last thing in the world I felt like doing was walking into a boardroom and facing my worst fears. But what could I do? I was absolutely committed.

After catching a ride to the hotel, I quickly changed into a suit and was off to the project kick-off meeting. While walking to the office from the hotel, I was thinking to myself how crazy it was that I had managed to dodge facing this fear for the past two years.

What happened to my fear during those two years of avoidance? It grew exponentially. By constantly finding ways to dodge this fear, I gave it more power. The fear became the number one situation in my life that I was constantly aware of and dodging. I really was more afraid of it than death. I know that sounds twisted, but that's how off kilter my perspective was. That's what can happen when you let anxiety get the best of you.

As I entered the boardroom and shook hands with my German counterparts, I was scared stiff. My heart was pounding as the round of introductions started.

Finally it was my turn. I swallowed hard and somehow managed to do it. It certainly wasn't my normal voice; it was as if I were just speaking with my breath, not vocal cords or body at all, but it sounded normal enough. No one seemed to notice how nervous I was, and then before I knew it, it was over.

Had I really tortured myself for two years over that? For those few seconds of speaking to a room full of strangers in a random conference room?

It was depressing as hell to think that was the situation, but it also gave me hope. I knew I could get through it again if I had to.

Once I settled into my new circumstances, a new routine in my life emerged. As the only single employee on the project, I was to spend almost all of my time on the road in Germany. That part I was actually looking forward to. . . at first. But after a few months, I realized this position wasn't the exciting opportunity I had thought it would be.

Often I was the only representative from our American firm at the client site in Germany. My role was as business analyst, acting as a liaison between the German client and our firm in Kansas City. This complex project had numerous technical difficulties that had to be figured out every single day. Unfortunately, this wasn't my area of expertise, as I was more business-focused and non-technical. Honestly speaking, I had little value to add at the client site.

In many European countries, besides consultants such as me, most employees rarely work a full forty-hour workweek. It doesn't matter what critical deadlines are looming, when they've put in their predefined required hours, they simply go home. Thus the office I worked in was often empty by 4:00 p.m.

In my office, the Germans would come to me with issues and concerns, which I would communicate to my colleagues in Kansas City. Due to the time difference, this meant that at 4:00 p.m. German time (9:00 a.m. Kansas City time), my second shift was just beginning.

My nights consisted of conference calls relaying information back to the team in Kansas City. Sometimes these calls lasted well past midnight.

Keeping this in mind, let me describe my living situation in Germany. I would stay at a decent hotel, get dressed for work, and then have breakfast in the dining room every morning—just me and a German newspaper. No one met me to have conversation. Most of the wait staff in the hotel were friendly first-generation immigrants from the Philippines. Getting to know them over the months while they poured my coffee each morning provided just enough face-to-face human interaction to keep me sane.

Then I'd head to work. I literally had no one to report to and rarely had a meeting to attend, so it could be extremely boring if I didn't have much work to do. Come lunchtime, I would head down to the swanky cafeteria. In this brand-new office building, the cafeteria boasted stylish decor, amazing food, and very attractive European women. Sounds like heaven for a single guy, right? That depends.

I still hadn't befriended anyone in the office, and even the Germans I worked directly with didn't invite me to join them, not for lunch, a beer after work, nothing. I thought it wasn't anything personal, rather it just seemed to be a cultural thing I observed while working in Germany. My only meal companion was whatever book I brought with me. No psychology degree is required to realize that this can't be good for the human psyche!

To sum it all up, I was living out of a hotel in Germany four out of every five weeks, working long hours and even weekends, and had no one with whom to spend my limited personal time. Not good.

More than a year had passed since I had graduated from the therapy group, but anxiety still greatly affected my life. My fears of public speaking and certain social situations were still in the back of my mind. I rarely had to attend meetings in person while in Germany; it was mostly just conference calls, which I could handle.

While I spent hours every evening on work-related phone calls, I really had no friends with whom to talk. I missed being with others and sharing face-to-face conversations. I hated work and became lonelier each day.

By that winter, I was completely burned out. I could feel the tension and stress building throughout my body. I had been a very physically active person who loved to go for runs and hit the gym. But now I was overweight and out of shape for the first time in many years. I needed clean air, exercise, and some fresh perspective. So along with a friend of mine who worked in England, I took a snowboarding trip to Bavaria.

I was excited to get back to the beautiful Alps, breathe the fresh air, and get some exercise while snowboarding in such a serene setting. Still, I did not like crowded and packed places, and I knew I would inevitably face a crowded gondola or lift to the top of the mountain. I didn't want that to stop me. I knew I really needed this trip.

As usual, we had more than our share of beers out on the town on Friday night, and I awoke in a mild hangover daze. I had wanted to avoid that, because I knew that being dehydrated exaggerates the symptoms associated with panic and anxiety. I had not only experienced this firsthand on numerous occasions while hung over but had also heard it from medical doctors. Knowing I was going to face a crowded gondola that morning in this state made me a nervous wreck.

As we finally got to the lift station, it was even worse than I had imagined. A line of more than 200 people stood ahead of us, and the gondolas were coming only every fifteen minutes or so. Once an empty gondola came down, it was jam-packed with more than fifty people for the ten-minute ride to the top. I had to run to the restroom twice while in line due to my nervous and upset stomach.

Each crowded gondola brought me closer to my inevitable turn to board. I had no confidence in myself in this difficult situation, and was already experiencing some overwhelming what-if thoughts. I paced nervously in circles, making small talk and joking with my buddy, trying to distract myself from the nightmare I was about to enter.

As it finally became our turn, I saw us as cows being shoved into a holding pen. The only thing missing were cattle prods. Desperately seeking a spot against one of the windows, I had to settle for the worst place for me—dead center in the now-jam-packed gondola. As the doors closed, I said a prayer under my breath.

Once we had been going for about twenty seconds, I looked back and saw that we had already gone a few hundred feet and were making quick progress. I then turned and followed the cables up the mountain and realized just how much farther we would have to go. More important, I realized how much longer I would be stuck in this claustrophobic sardine can of people.

I'm sure you know what's coming next: a panic attack. My heart was absolutely pounding out of my chest. I nervously shuffled my feet around and tried to slow my breathing. I looked around for some way to get rid of this surge of nervous energy. I saw a support bar that ran across the ceiling of the gondola, just above my head. I almost jumped up and started doing pull-ups, seriously! Picture a group of reserved and polite Europeans crammed into a gondola staring at some stupid American (me) who's yelling and doing pull-ups! What a sight that would have been.

I tried to find a way to distract myself. Finally I just turned to my buddy and said something completely random and stupid and out of the blue. "Think we'll run into those girls we met at the bar last night?" It worked. We began to have a pointless conversation, and it was enough to distract and calm me down. Not more than two minutes after the panic attack, I was fine. I knew I couldn't have another one anytime soon. I had already peaked and was now in the aftershock feeling of it all. My legs were barely able to hold me up.

As we approached the mountain peak and the end of the gondola ride, I was actually enjoying it. I was able to see past the supposed danger and scariness of this crowded space. I gazed at the breathtaking Alpine mountain scenery I had come to view and experience and was glad I had come on this trip. I knew when I made plans for it that I would have to face what I just did, and I hadn't let it stop me. I wanted this vacation so badly that I was willing to face this scary situation to get it.

After enjoying a perfect day on the slopes, I still had something looming over my head: the gondola ride back down the mountain. I had tried to block it out and just enjoy my day on the slopes, but I was very concerned about it the entire day. Having experienced a panic attack in the same gondola just six hours earlier, I reluctantly boarded it a second time.

As the doors closed and we started on our way, my anxiety washed back over me like a wave. Although I was stuck and panicking internally, I showed no signs. Despite telling myself I was going to lose it, I didn't. I mean, this was the worst of the worst, folks. I was tired physically and mentally, dehydrated from partying the night before, and had been worrying about getting back in this gondola the whole day. Yet I made it through. I was a little shaken when we reached the bottom, but I was okay. My second ride proved to be much easier than my first one earlier that morning.

By the spring of 2005, I was beyond miserable with my job. Sure, I was making great money and was abroad again, but I had no social life whatsoever. I was frustrated and uninterested in the work I was doing, although I did my job well.

KNOW WHEN TO FOLD 'EM

While I felt physically isolated, there was always a place I could find some social interaction—the Internet. During that long winter, over countless hours alone on my computer, I discovered online poker. I know what you're thinking, but let me explain.

Because I had little time to socialize away from my computer, poker became my only outlet. It became more than a hobby, it became a passion—a passion with a lot of potential.

I became extremely motivated. I wanted out of my current work situation, and the potential of making a lot of money from poker enticed me. I wanted to buy my freedom. So, I studied every poker book I could get my hands on and played daily for hours on end.

Let me make a long story short. By that March, I was making more money at poker than I was at my job. A lot more. Considering how miserable my job made me feel and all the good parts of life I felt I was missing out on, my decision was clear. I quit my job to play poker for a living that spring.

Playing online poker was a welcome break from the structured and stiff working environment I hated. I was so happy not having to face an office and deal with meetings and other situations that made me very uncomfortable. As my own boss, I was making more money than I ever had in my life. I felt free. I could sleep all day if I wanted, go to the beach, eat anywhere I wanted, and work whenever I wanted. The summer was off to a great start!

Then the isolation really started to bother me. My friends in Chicago still had to go to work every day. They still had a structured workday with meetings and deadlines, so I had no one to even talk to during the day.

Co-workers? No such thing in this profession. When you're working from home, your only interaction is an occasional chat conversation with another player at the poker table whose money you're trying to take, so it's not exactly friendly. I began to feel more and more isolated as days went by, which really affected my mental health. Somehow I had created the same situation I had experienced in Germany: social isolation and lack of stimulation.

Sure I had tons of free time and was in great physical shape, but I had no relationships. I could have joined groups or volunteered or something, but I didn't. This was because my old anxieties I thought I had overcome a year earlier were starting to creep back into my life. With no one pushing me or telling me I had to do anything, my motivation to face my anxiety-related problems had disappeared.

Why should I go and ride the el or a crowded bus? I never needed to, especially at rush hour. Why should I go to Toastmasters and face my public-speaking fears? I didn't have to speak at meetings anymore, I could just sit at home and click a mouse and make a bunch of money.

By the end of the summer, I was a mess. The progress that I had made overcoming anxiety was gone. My confidence was severely shaken, and I knew once again that I needed to make some major changes. Unfortunately for my bank account, my dazed psyche began to affect the quality of my poker play. A key to success in poker is having a level head and not letting your emotions get the best of you. My emotions were all over the place, and that spells disaster when you've got thousands of dollars at stake at any given second.

The emotional and financial roller coaster of professional poker is too hard for most people to take, and I was no exception. These swings only pushed my anxieties further. By the end of the summer, I had lost most of the money I had built up from my poker play. Now financially hurting in addition to my mental woes, I was in a pretty sad state.

The worst part was not that I gave playing poker for a living a shot and didn't make it. To me, that wasn't a huge deal. I was anguished, because I now knew that I would have to return to an office job. I would have to face big, stiff, weekly status meetings again. I would have to relive my nightmare scenarios. Although I had faced down some of my fears before, my confidence was gone and I was back at rock bottom again.

Reluctantly, I contacted a former boss in Chicago. She happily offered me a position, and that fall, I was a working stiff once again.

RETURN TO THE LAND OF CUBICLES

I was beyond depressed when I returned to the cubicle jungle. I had just come from a summer of complete freedom in which I had no structure and was never forced to be in any uncomfortable situations. Now I had to face them every day. No one had depended upon me for anything, and I was never examined under the microscope. My co-workers had been my computer and my money.

Readjusting to office life was difficult, and I felt on edge for the first few months. Furthermore, the work itself was monotonous and uninspiring, which frustrated me further.

I was avoiding any and all situations that had made me anxious in the past. I wasn't dating, only rode uncrowded buses to and from work, and completely avoided the el.

Feeling very low and desperate for help, I began to read some of the self-help books I had stockpiled over the years. I even took out my old notebook from my anxiety class again and reviewed it. I was starting to remember the feelings of triumph I had when I had faced down my fears of the el and my panic attacks. I finally became so frustrated with what I had let my life once again become that I decided I would start my recovery over again.

DO-OVER

I had relapsed and found myself back where I had started two years earlier. However, this time there was a difference. I knew what I needed to do to get my confidence back. I began the same way as before, riding the el at lunch when it was least crowded.

Over that next winter, I stayed committed. I graduated to riding the el home from work during crowded rush hours. I remember one particular day standing in a packed train car stopped in between stations. I smiled as I thought to myself, "Wow, I know I'm fine. I couldn't have a panic attack right now if I tried." I have to tell you, there isn't a more empowering feeling in the world than to know you have conquered such a tremendous fear.

By January, I was feeling great and even went on a snowboarding trip to Lake Tahoe with a few good friends. If you'll recall, during my last ski trip a year earlier in Germany, I had experienced a panic attack. It happened while I was riding a crowded gondola to the top of the mountain. This scarring memory was in the back of my mind as we planned the Tahoe trip.

The time came, and I boarded a gondola. I was very anxious, probably at an anxiety level of 75 out of 100. But thirty seconds or so into the ride, I just took in the beauty of the scenery and began to smile. I was fine. I had faced down the fear. Now it was time to enjoy the mountain scenery and have a blast with my buddies. We enjoyed the trip, and I remember feeling so relaxed and rejuvenated on the plane ride home.

As the spring came, I was feeling good about myself. Panic attacks were honestly the last thing on my mind. I still had my fears of public speaking, but since I rarely had to face them, I didn't spend much time thinking about them. Like most people, I just told myself that someday, when I'm feeling better, I'll face my fears.

In early summer, I began to receive some disturbing family news from my mother back home. As this is my family's business, I won't go into details, but I will say that I couldn't sleep for days after I learned about these things. I felt helpless being so far away from home.

Now that I fully understood the severity of the problems at home, I was on edge. Any time I saw that a family member was calling, my heart sank as I answered the call, expecting the worst.

I became a derailed train of fear and anxiety. My nerves were frayed, and I was constantly worrying about the situation at home. As I grew more and more anxious, it revived some of the panic feelings I thought I had put to rest. One day, riding the el home after work, things reached a boiling point.

I had another panic attack on the el, something that hadn't happened in almost two years. I exited the train at the next stop, completely shaken. The next day I tried to prove my panic wrong by boarding the el again, but instead I talked myself into another panic attack. Looking back now, I know I would have been okay had I just stuck it out and stayed on the train, but I exited after going only one stop. That was it. I was back to where I had started... again.

Now that the el was once again off limits for me, I returned to taking buses to and from work. But it wasn't long before even taking buses also caused me great distress. Several minor panic episodes on crowded buses were added blows.

The tricky part about panic and anxiety is it may take just one particular event to shake your confidence in all areas of your life. Now that I was terrified of riding the el again, other problems that hadn't been there for a long time started to creep back in.

Given that it was summer in Chicago (offering endless opportunities for fun), I tried to enjoy myself. But I was holding back, ever fearful of another panic attack or embarrassing situation. I remember a dinner date I had with a girl at an outdoor restaurant. I started to get anxious and panicky. I remember the fear I had that I might get up and sprint away from the table. My what-if thinking was running my mind again. Even a casual date with a cute girl was terrifying.

At this point, I just about gave up on dating. My life was in emotional shambles, although no one around me would have known. After going through this for years, I had become quite the actor. Then I had a new problem to deal with.

One of my best friends asked me to be in his wedding in September. This large wedding had an international flair to it with many people coming from abroad. It would be held in one of the most crowded and anxiety-filled places in the world: New York City.

Now that my panic attacks were back and any pressure situation made me cringe, I dreaded being in this wedding from the moment my friend asked me. Don't get me wrong, I was very honored and happy for him, but my anxiety had once again come to rule my life.

In a last ditch effort to overcome my fears of being in front of a crowd, I psyched myself up enough to attend a Toastmasters meeting. Attending was something I had put off for years and had only tried once before.

The only previous meeting I had attended had been a year earlier at a different chapter in Chicago. I'll never forget pacing in the hallway near the meeting room, deciding whether or not I would actually go in. Eventually I did, and I couldn't believe I was actually walking into my worst fear. Before the meeting started, the club president approached the guests sitting in the back and asked if we wanted to introduce ourselves.

Despite my pounding heart, I knew this was why I had come to the meeting, so I agreed. To my surprise, I got through my introduction just fine. Unfortunately, I hadn't attended another Toastmasters meeting since.

Now, however, I was really feeling the pressure of the upcoming wedding. I had four months before the ceremony and figured if I attended the Toastmasters meetings regularly, I could overcome my fears of being in front of a crowd and would be fine for the wedding.

I was nervous for weeks before my first meeting, but eventually the day came and I did well. This time I told myself I would stick it out and keep going to meetings.

After attending meetings for a few consecutive weeks, I scheduled myself to get up and give a real speech. My mind was flooded with memories of the panic attack I had in the German training class while trying to speak. Still, I had to press on.

As I took the stage, I spontaneously told the audience how hard it was for me to be giving a speech, and that "I'd rather bungee jump off of the Sears Tower than be up there speaking!" This got the group laughing, but it was the truth. They knew I was speaking from the heart, for I was noticeably nervous, but it didn't matter. My anxiety dropped dramatically once I got going. No longer than fifteen or twenty seconds into my speech, I was coasting and feeling confident.

When I finished my speech, I received a wonderfully supportive round of applause. I sat down, and a wave of complete relief, elation, and accomplishment washed over me. I had a perm-a-grin that couldn't be removed from my face. At the end of the meeting, the toastmaster asked me how I thought I did on my speech, using a ranking of one to ten (with ten being the best possible rating). I told them I thought my speech was a nine, but for facing my fears, I gave myself a twenty!

Because I had done so well, I got a bit cocky and justified skipping subsequent Toastmasters meetings.

Before I knew it, the wedding was only a month away, and I was an anxious disaster. Pat from my Toastmasters group sent me an e-mail out of the blue inviting me to participate in a humorous speech contest. With nothing to lose, I decided to go for it and signed up.

Only two of us competed, but that didn't make me any less nervous. Having given my first speech successfully just a few months earlier made this one easier. I won the contest and felt good, but I realized something that night. When I started my speech that evening, I was once again extremely nervous and almost panicking. However, just twenty seconds or so into it, I was fine. If I had been going to the meetings all summer, by then I would have been much more comfortable in front of a group of people. But I hadn't, and I still felt extremely unprepared for the upcoming wedding.

With about a week to go before the wedding, I was a dead man walking. I felt like I could pop at any moment. My stomach was constantly killing me, and I wasn't sleeping well. I was back to drinking at least a six-pack every night by myself. I tried to convince myself that I would be okay, that I had gotten through two speeches recently and had done just fine. But deep down my negative thoughts and beliefs told me otherwise. By now it was far too late to fix my problems in time for the wedding. I had a plane to catch.

Heading to the airport the morning of my flight, I had a hangover and was tired as hell, having been up late worrying about all that awaited me in New York. As I had a full day ahead of me, I wanted to snap out of my daze on the flight and hit the ground running in Manhattan. After all, we didn't have anything but fun stuff planned for the first two nights (this was Wednesday, the wedding was Saturday). So, I ordered my usual double-shot latte in the airport and waited for my plane.

I was very anxious thinking about standing up in front of more than 200 well-educated and successful New Yorkers and well-traveled foreigners. Knowing how formal and traditional the ceremony would be made me dread it even more. I remember as the plane took off and I was looking out the window at Lake Michigan and the coastline below, my worries swelled out of control. Planes had never bothered me before, even when I was at my worst with panic attacks. But like it or not, I was going to have to face one.

Before I knew it, ladies and gentlemen—panic attack time. Some of the fun thoughts in my mind include such hits as:

- "I have to be on this plane for two-and-a-half more hours. I'll never make it!"
- "What if I go over and rip the door open? What would stop me from doing something like that?"
- "What if I start freaking out and running up and down the aisles and can't calm myself down? They'll have to restrain me and lock me up, and I'll be arrested when I get to New York. I won't make the wedding, and I'll be a complete embarrassment to everyone. I'll ruin the wedding and my friend's whole marriage!"
- "What if I repeatedly run as hard as I can into the cockpit door trying to break in? I'll be arrested and everyone will think I'm a terrorist!"

I started to think that there was no way I could make it through the wedding. I'd have to call my friend once we landed in New York (if I even made it through this flight without bringing down the plane!) and make up some insane excuse. As the flight continued, I eventually calmed down somewhat. I was extremely frazzled and exhausted. I ordered a scotch, slammed it, and slowly returned to somewhat normal anxiety levels, or at least normal for me.

The two days before the wedding were fun, but I never really let myself fully enjoy them. I was still worried about what loomed over my head, the ceremony itself. We explored the city and enjoyed much of the trip, but the inevitable had come.

The night before the wedding, I opted not to go out on the town with the rest of the wedding party. I knew how much more anxious and awful I would feel while hung over and dehydrated, and I wanted to give myself the best possible chance of surviving this event. I tossed and turned all night and probably got a few hours of sleep. The dread and stress was unbearable. I couldn't wait for it to be over.

So what ended up happening? Guess.

After the ceremony began, I did start to have a mild panic attack while standing before the crowd, but I smiled and fought through it with my breathing and muscle relaxation techniques. It is surprising that it didn't scare me; in fact, I was more annoyed by it.

Just a few minutes into the ceremony, I began to smile and enjoy the moment. One of my best friends was getting married. I saw some familiar faces in the crowd, lots of smiles, and was able to finally enjoy this beautiful moment. Now why the hell couldn't it have been like this for the past few months? Aaaarrrggghhh!

So as was the case with any other event I've built up in my mind as the end-all be-all most important thing that I can't screw up, I passed with flying colors. You'd figure I would have learned my lesson by now, right?

I still had the flight home ahead of me, but that was easy for one particular reason. Admittedly still drunk from partying all night, I boarded an 8:00 a.m. flight for Chicago. Before we even finished taxiing to the runway, I was passed out cold. Guess that's one way to deal with anxiety, lol.

The amount of relief I felt after getting through the wedding is indescribable. Something I had dreaded for nearly a year was over. Throughout my life I've found that the stress and tension I put my body through in such circumstances can often take weeks or even months to flush itself out. This wedding was no exception.

I had planned to begin putting my life back together once the wedding was over, but now that it was done I felt overwhelmed with depression. One random morning, I had a panic attack on a bus bound for work. Here we go again.

BOTTOMED OUT

I remember the day clearly. It was November, and I had called in sick to work, but not because I was truly sick. I just felt like avoiding the world that day.

I needed a haircut badly, so I figured I'd get that out of the way. For years I'd been getting my hair cut by Franco, a popular Sicilian barber in my neighborhood. On the weekends, you may wait two hours or more to see him. Since I was home for the day, I figured I'd get it out of the way. Plus, I wouldn't have to face the huge weekend crowd I dreaded.

Just before leaving my apartment, I started to envision having a panic attack in the barber chair and what a disaster it would be. How embarrassing it would be to do that in front of a room full of other men and the barbers whom I had befriended. I began to have a panic attack right there in my living room just thinking about it! This was it, folks, my rock bottom, definitely the lowest point in my life. I had surpassed my previous anxiety levels by so much that I was now having a panic attack by myself in my own apartment! I was in the most comforting and safe setting possible—in my home by myself—and I was still completely freaking out.

This was the final straw. With tears in my eyes, I vowed to myself and to God that I was going to get my life back. I was tired of what my life had become, and I was going to fight back. I felt awful, completely beaten down by the world and my own fears. I was not going to be denied my life, and I was not going to give up. Although I was out of self-confidence and didn't believe in myself any more, there was still something deep inside of me that refused to give up. Terrified but walking with purpose, I made my way to the barbershop.

While walking, I told myself, "I know I'm a disaster right now, but I'm tired of my fears pushing me around. I'm going to run right into the roar of the lion and pick a fight!"

And so I did. I was as anxious as I had ever been in my life sitting there in the barber's chair. My heart rate had to be more than 150 beats per minute as Franco put the plastic sheet around me. But I said to myself over and over again, "I'm not going to run. I'm staying right here," as I lowered myself into the seat a little further, signaling to myself that, like it or not, I was staying.

It took ten minutes in the barber's chair for me to finally calm down and realize I wasn't going to panic—ten minutes of hell followed by a wave of relief.

I felt something I hadn't felt in a long time. I felt hope again.

PART II

LEARNING
THE LESSONS

LEARNING
THE LESSONS

IN PART I, I TOLD YOU ABOUT my struggles with anxiety
and panic. I was very lost for a very long time. To help myself, I
read many books, listened to inspirational audio programs, and
even participated in therapy sessions to find relief.

During this research, I gained a deeper understanding. I made
wonderful changes in my life, both physically and mentally.
I experimented with various mental exercises and practices,
exposed myself to my fears, and (sometimes!) learned from my
mistakes. After a while, I achieved a sort of awakening in which my
anxiety problems finally made sense.

While the journey was incredibly strenuous, it was also very
rewarding. What I will do in Part II is to share the insights and
the knowledge I have gained in the most valuable way—not from
psychology courses at a university or from talking to a bunch of
doctors, but rather, through my personal experiences.

SO WHAT IS A PANIC ATTACK?

Let's start off with some education and scientifically define a "panic attack." According to WebMD:

> *"A panic attack is a sudden bout of intense fear or anxiety that causes frightening but not life-threatening symptoms such as a pounding heart, shortness of breath, and the feeling of losing control or dying. Usually from five to twenty minutes long, a panic attack may be triggered by stressful circumstances or it may occur unexpectedly."*
>
> (www.webmd.com/anxiety-panic/tc/panic-attacks-and-panic-disorder-topic-overview; Article: "Panic Attacks and Panic Disorder—Topic Overview")

Seems like a logical description. For the purpose of this book, you might also find my own definition useful:

> *"A panic attack is a really scary feeling that you are going to die, have a heart attack, or completely lose control and start flipping out and going crazy. After you've had one, it changes your life. Panic attacks can send you into a downward spiral of depression, shame, guilt, embarrassment, hopelessness, virtual insanity, self-medication, and agoraphobia."*

Before I really depress you, let me continue:

> *"Panic attacks may also bring out the very best in you, humanize and humble you, and allow you to reach higher levels of self-confidence and consciousness that you never thought possible. They can help motivate you to right your course in the sea of life and regain balance."*

Let me tell you something important: You're not crazy. You're not losing your mind. You're probably not going to act out any of the scary thoughts that keep replaying in your mind. In all of my scary panic-attack moments, I never acted out any of the crazy thoughts I had.

Believe it or not, these frightening ideas that sometimes fill your mind were actually put there by you. Of course, you didn't mean to put them there, just as I didn't mean to do the same to myself. But take solace in this—if you put them there, you can also remove them.

> *"Most of the shadows of this life are caused by our standing in our own sunshine."*
>
> RALPH WALDO EMERSON
> (American writer, poet, philosopher, and leader of the Transcendentalist movement in the nineteenth century)

Are you turning green?

Physically speaking, it's actually simple what's happening to you during a panic attack. As intelligent as humans are, we still have many primal instincts of self-preservation and survival ingrained in us. We have a response system built into our psyche that is involuntarily activated when our mind tells us that we are in danger.

This response is referred to as fight-or-flight. Our body releases stimulants and adrenalin into the bloodstream, causing the heart to race, hair to stand up on the back of the neck, muscles to tense, and we begin to perspire. Why? The mind has signaled to the body, "We're in some serious trouble here, and we have to fight or flee if we want to survive!"

The body becomes over-stimulated and ready to fight for its survival. But why do we experience each specific symptom? The reasons are as follows:

- Your body releases sugars and adrenalin into the blood for added strength and speed.
- Your heart pounds to spread this energy-rich blood to muscles throughout the body.
- Perspiration forms on your skin, making it difficult for would-be predators to grasp you.
- Your hair stands up on end to make you appear larger and more intimidating to an attacker or predator.

This innate human ability has astounding positive potential, such as when a sixty-year-old grandmother lifts a 3,000-pound burning car to save the lives of her grandchildren. This remarkable system allows the human body to do truly miraculous things under extreme distress.

While growing up, the television series *The Incredible Hulk* was one of my favorite shows. The premise was that the main character had tried to harness the tremendous fight-or-flight power all humans possess so he could use it at will. The experiment went terribly wrong, and he was exposed to an overdose of stimulant chemicals and radiation. The result was that he was unable to control his fight-or-flight response, and his symptoms were many times stronger than a normal man's.

This poor guy was thus doomed to spend his life running from confrontations and anything that would upset him. Why? Because once he became agitated in any way, it triggered his fight-or-flight mechanism, which caused him to turn into a green 300-pound, muscle-bound behemoth. He would freak out and throw cars, run through walls, and so on.

If panic attacks worked like that, they'd actually be a lot more entertaining, wouldn't they? I doubt I would have sought help! I'd probably be touring the country now, performing feats of strength at some sideshow.

During a panic attack, you are essentially awakening your own inner "Incredible Hulk" at very inappropriate times. How did this come to be? Over time, your mind and thought processes have become skewed to an extreme degree. You are interpreting situations that make you uncomfortable as dangerous and a threat to your survival. Your mind is telling your body that it is fighting for its survival when you encounter such situations.

Once your body starts to go into its fight-or-flight mode, the physical symptoms frighten you even more. You feel as if you are no longer in control of your body. You wonder what you will do with this huge surge of emotional and physical energy, and your mind fills with scary possibilities and negative worries. You wonder if you'll actually act out some of these thoughts, which scares you even further. Soon your horrible, crazy thoughts are racing just as fast as your heartbeat. Behold… a panic attack.

The good news is that the body cannot stay this over-stimulated for very long. According to the National Institute of Mental Health, a panic attack usually peaks within ten minutes, while the symptoms may last longer. (www.nimh.nih.gov/health/publications/anxiety-disorders/panic-disorder.shtml; Article: "Panic Disorder")

In my experiences, however, my panic attacks rarely lasted longer than thirty seconds. This doesn't mean that I wasn't anxious or feeling on edge for minutes or even hours leading up to or following the actual panic attack. Rather, it means that when all of my emotions came to a head and I peaked, it didn't last longer than thirty seconds. I estimate that most of my panic attacks lasted under ten seconds. Albeit ten lousy seconds!

You see, it's not the actual panic attack that's difficult; rather, it's the anticipation and fear of a panic attack that fuels your anxiety. This is where agoraphobia comes into the picture. Agoraphobia is defined as:

> *"An anxiety disorder, often precipitated by the fear of having a panic attack in a setting from which there is no easy means of escape. As a result, sufferers of agoraphobia may avoid public and/or unfamiliar places. In severe cases, the sufferer may become confined to their home, experiencing difficulty traveling from this 'safe place.'"*
>
> (http://en.wikipedia.org/wiki/Agoraphobia)

Even if I tell you that the worst panic attacks won't last longer than thirty seconds, the pessimist in you may respond, "Sure, most last less than thirty seconds, but what if I am the extreme case? What if I have one that lasts longer? I am such an anxious mess that I know I could have one that will last for hours!"

Listen. I am telling you from my own experience that what you fear most—a true panic attack—only lasts for a very short time.

Why am I doing this?

Believe it or not, you are causing yourself to have panic attacks in your best interest. That's not a typo, I'm serious. You are having panic attacks for a very good reason.

Your interpretations of experiences throughout your life and other influences have conditioned you to form beliefs about everything. For example, you believe if you stare at the sun it will damage your eyes. Your parents and doctors have probably told you this, but more important you know this to be true because you have stared at the sun. You have personally felt the pain it inflicts on your eyes. This belief has been reinforced by your own experiences. Thus, you hold it to be a fact that staring at the sun is indeed harmful to your eyes.

Now let's analyze something common to many panic sufferers, a fear of being in a situation in which they perceive they are physically trapped. Let's use the example of driving in heavy traffic on an expressway that crosses over a long bridge. This may be an activity that you've done hundreds of times and has become routine.

One particular morning, you weren't feeling well. You were overwhelmed with stress and worry about a bad relationship, money problems, or some upcoming event. The constant honking and anger of the other drivers was feeding your frustration and distress. As you sat there in the gridlocked traffic approaching the bridge, something new and different happened. Your mind began to race as your built-up stress and anxiety reached a boiling point and began to spill over. You had a panic attack right there in your car while stuck in traffic on the bridge.

You had nowhere to go. You were very scared, but after a few minutes you managed to calm down. You made it across the bridge upset, but still alive.

Now what happens? You may associate panic and fear with traffic and crossing bridges. You start to think that everything associated with your experience that morning is bad because you now have your experience as evidence. This evidence reinforces your thoughts until they become beliefs, and beliefs are powerful things. They shape your world and define what you can and cannot do, for better or worse.

You now believe that driving in heavy traffic over a bridge is a threatening setting. Your experience that one fateful morning is proof, which provides reinforcement and makes your belief even stronger. Now you avoid this situation, because you see it as a threat to your well-being and happiness.

As you associate pain and fear with a situation, your mind signals your body to be on guard. If that situation arises, your survival mechanisms may be triggered. These mechanisms take the form of the uncomfortable symptoms associated with a panic attack— rapid heartbeat, shaky and over-stimulated muscles, restlessness, and sweat. Your body launches the fight-or-flight response to your thoughts about this particular situation.

Do you need these primal survival mechanisms to survive driving in heavy traffic or being stuck in a crowded elevator? No, of course you don't! Unfortunately your body doesn't know the difference. Because of your beliefs, you have programmed your mind that being stuck in traffic on a bridge is just as dangerous and threatening to your survival as being cornered by a hungry dinosaur in a cave.

You are the one who put this belief into place and gave it power. But don't despair—the good news is that you can also take that power away. You created the problem, yet you also hold its solution within you at this very moment.

The standard progression of anxiety and panic disorder

My panic attacks were caused by several factors, but what really fed them were the negative thoughts that flourished in my mind. In talking with many others who have suffered from panic attacks, we noticed a typical cycle of events.

1) **You have your first panic attack.** This causes an unbelievable amount of distress and heartache. You have no idea what is happening to you.

    I remember after my first one, the next few days I was still completely frazzled thinking, "What the hell was that?" Even more troubling was the question, "Is it going to happen again?"

2) **Your world begins to shrink.** You are on edge hoping another panic attack doesn't come. You start to think about your daily life and all of the situations in which having a panic attack would be catastrophic. Mundane tasks such as riding in a car with others, sitting in traffic, taking a crowded elevator, taking public transportation, sitting in meetings in the workplace, and so on. These are now threats to you, so you avoid them. Your fear of another panic attack has a stranglehold on you and governs your life. You will do anything to avoid the embarrassment of having a panic attack in front of someone else.

3) **Your battered self-confidence fades.** This is an especially cruel part of panic disorder, one that affects all areas of your life.

    For me, I lost almost all confidence in things that I had been very good at throughout my life. I found that any type of performance anxiety I previously had experienced was amplified to an extreme degree.

4) **Agoraphobia sets in.** You may be feeling mentally and emotionally broken. You don't do anything that causes you to leave your comfort zone whatsoever, unless you are forced to. Even then, you come up with creative ways to avoid such situations.

    For me, just going to work every day was a nightmare. I'd lie in bed dreading the next morning's bus ride to work, and the ultimate horror—the possibility of being pulled into a meeting and having to speak in front of others. After work, I went straight home. I didn't want to go out and socialize anymore. I didn't want to risk being in any scary or unpredictable situations in which I might embarrass myself.

5) **You try self-medication.** This involves indulging in any type of substance to calm down and attempt to forget your troubled thoughts.

    My choice was alcohol. Although I certainly entertained the idea of drinking at work, I didn't cross that line. My consumption was limited to binging nightly by myself just to help quiet my racing mind. For years, I felt I needed several beers just to fall asleep.

6) **You try prescription medication.** Still unsure of what is happening to you, you go to the doctor. Having no true solution for you, doctors will often prescribe an antidepressant to help relieve your symptoms. Some people do see an immediate improvement.

    Despite trying many prescription antidepressants, I still managed to have panic attacks. It was clear medication wasn't going to solve my problems. I knew something else must be behind my behavior.

7) **You search for your own answers.** Now here's where the story starts to change. You are assuming more responsibility by taking matters into your own hands, and this is positive. This is what led you to this book. Your hunger for freedom and demand for a better quality of life have motivated you. First off, good for you! You are on the brink of a great accomplishment.

   This journey requires extensive self-exploration and open-mindedness. You have to be honest with yourself and identify the weaknesses and problems you've chosen to ignore. Now is the time to face and overcome them.

WHY I THINK WE HAVE RELAPSES

Over the course of a few years, I had overcome some of my worst fears multiple times, only to have them reappear with even greater strength. Why?

What had gone wrong? How could I have gone from nearly forgetting about panic attacks to constantly agonizing over having one while getting a haircut, going to a restaurant or sharing a cab with friends?

Just as panic and anxiety are very complex, the answers are as well. Now that time has passed, and I'm a little older and somewhat wiser, I can look back objectively. Here are some key mistakes that led to my relapses.

Lesson #1: Finish the job.

I knew deep down that I wasn't fully facing my fears and giving it my all. Being such a driven person in so many other areas of my life, why didn't I just follow through? The answer: I was too afraid.

I felt like I had done enough. It's human nature to resist change, and I fell right into that trap. I became complacent.

On multiple occasions, I overcame my panic attacks, which was quite a feat considering how bad they had been. I was able to take flights and ride crowded trains, buses, and cabs without even thinking twice. However triumphant I felt, a monster lurked in my closet that I attempted to ignore: performance anxiety.

Performance anxiety takes many forms. You may fear speaking in front of a group, playing a sport before a crowd, or even just walking past a group of onlookers. For some people, signing a check at the cashier with a line of people behind them is nerve racking. Many people are comfortable performing various activities until you put them before an audience. The audience may consist of one person or many, many more. The root of this anxiety is the fear of disapproval.

Let me expand on this. I have a scientific background (engineering), and I like to approach problems analytically. I studied extensively to learn what I could about panic attacks. I wanted to know my enemy so I would know how to defeat it. **A simple fact that became clear to me was that a panic attack could not kill me.** It might wreak havoc on my psyche and nerves and upset my stomach, but it is no physical threat to my survival whatsoever.

So why was I so afraid of them? It turns out I wasn't. I was afraid of *what people would think of me* if I had one in front of them. My fear was that people would think I was crazy or weird, and reject or disapprove of me.

I felt that my friends would no longer want to hang out with me. Women would surely be frightened and never want to date me. Co-workers would think I was crazy, and I'd probably lose my job. I thought if I freaked out in the wrong place, such as on a plane, I might be arrested and suddenly I'd be a criminal! (What would my poor mother think?)

When I previously thought I had beaten my panic, I had only overcome one specific aspect of my fear of disapproval—panicking in a confined or inescapable space. I had beaten this fear twice, but my confidence didn't last. I had ignored my performance anxiety.

The problem was that I still had many other situations in which my fear of disapproval had not been addressed. Doing anything in front of a crowd, even playing a friendly game of kickball in a fun co-ed league with friends caused me tremendous fear and anxiety.

I needed to face the fears I had been suppressing and had hoped would go away on their own. I couldn't just overcome one fear and hope that the others would magically disappear. I had to face them all.

> *"Ultimately we know deeply that the other side of every fear is a freedom."*
>
> Marilyn Ferguson
> (best-selling author of *The Brain Revolution*)

Lesson #2: Get your ass in shape!

Throughout my life, anytime I've allowed my physical fitness to slip, it's caused problems. My self-confidence dropped because I didn't feel strong or energetic, and I'd easily get out of breath while performing simple tasks such as walking up a flight of stairs. Because I hadn't been regularly exerting myself and strengthening my heart through cardiovascular exercise, my rapid heartbeat, a symptom of my panic, seemed unfamiliar and scary.

When I'm in good physical shape, however, my life improves. Because I'm exercising regularly, my heart is stronger. If I become anxious, it takes more anxiety to raise my heart rate, thus making my symptoms less frightening.

When I'm fit, I feel more confident and walk upright with a self-assured posture, signaling to the world (and myself) that I feel strong. Feeling well physically is directly related to the mental image I carry of myself.

Working out also helps regulate my sleeping patterns. I fall asleep more easily when I've exercised that day. Think about what parents do with their hyperactive little kids. They let them run around and wear themselves out so they'll collapse from exhaustion and sleep soundly at night. I've found it's harder to have a panic attack when I've already burned off my excess energy through exercise. And just like a kid, if I've worn myself out, I sleep more soundly at night.

Last, there is certainly a release that is often referred to as a "high" one experiences after a great workout. Anytime I've felt extremely stressed out and anxious, I make it a point to run, cycle, and lift weights. How the stress and tension melt away when I am finished!

Through any physically demanding activity, the body releases endorphins, which make me feel good. And feeling good is the key to all of this.

Lesson #3: Don't eat like a Viking!

Something else I correlated with my worst anxiety periods was poor diet. I had stopped cooking healthy meals at home and instead opted for ordering salty and fatty takeout food. With my stomach already sensitive and reactive due to my constant worrying, I spent entirely too much time feeling lousy, seated in the bathroom.

Additionally, most U.S. restaurants give you oversized portions, often so huge that if you're coming close to finishing them, you're eating way too much. I would often feel bloated and tired after a meal. Even when eating healthy, controlling portion size is important.

What I've found works best for me is a diet consisting of lean protein (poultry and fish), whole grains (not too many empty carbohydrates such as white bread, fries, potato chips, or bagels), low sugar, and plenty of vitamins through drinking natural juices. I also try to eat at least one piece of fruit per day.

I have noticed that I feel best when I'm physically lean. My body functions more efficiently when I'm in shape and sleeping well. I still indulge in a great dessert every now and then or order a triple bacon heart-attack burger and fries. I just limit such splurges.

Last, I drink a lot of water and stay well hydrated. If I'm running errands or am out of pocket for a few hours and haven't been drinking much water, my energy level drops substantially. Proper hydration also helps to cleanse your body and flush out the toxins.

Lesson #4: Drink caffeine in moderation.

I absolutely love good, strong coffee. When I experienced its full potential while living in Europe, I was hooked. To keep me going at the monotonous office jobs I've held since college, coffee became a necessity.

While caffeine helps to wake you up, it has some negative effects, too. First and foremost, caffeine is a stimulant. If you analyze your worst panic attacks, you may find that you had caffeine that day. For me, it acted as a catalyst and intensified some of my worst attacks. The panic attack I had during the flight to New York for my friend's wedding was certainly aided by the double-shot latte I had before boarding.

When I'm particularly anxious, I simply cut back on caffeine. I know this is difficult, especially if you have a tedious job or task to do. However, I found a couple of alternatives that have helped me. Most coffee shops now offer chai tea lattes. They have far less caffeine than an espresso-based latte, and they're still served warm with milk, have some body to them, and can be a good substitute for your usual latte or coffee fix. I even bought a teapot and brew my own chai tea at work, mixing it with low fat milk. The tea provides a pick-me-up and is still satisfying.

Another alternative is to simply drink decaffeinated beverages. Caffeine-free sodas and coffees are so well made these days, you may not be able to tell the difference.

Anytime you are struggling with panic attacks, reduce the amount of caffeine and sugar you take in. Every little bit helps.

Lesson #5: Oktoberfest is once a year for a reason.

Alcohol seemingly numbs your senses and helps you forget your problems. When oppressive levels of anxiety and depression are reached, many people can't imagine not drinking alcohol to help quiet their worrisome thoughts.

The classic scene of a depressed person sitting alone in his or her apartment drinking a six-pack every night reflects some people's reality. Alcohol isn't the only form of self-medication, however.

My friends and I would go binge drinking to the point of complete stupidity. Why would I do this? I used it as an escape from the grim reality of dealing with my negative thoughts. The catch with alcohol is that hangovers are an extremely depressive state. I felt absolutely awful, drained, depressed, and the dehydration worsened my anxious feelings.

The first time I told a psychiatrist in the United States about a particular panic attack I had, he asked me if I had been dehydrated. I told him I had because I was extremely hung over from a late night of partying. He mentioned that it is very common to feel anxious and out of sorts while dehydrated. In addition, he said that these physical symptoms often compound anxious feelings.

So what did I do to change? Did I stop going out with my friends? At first, I did. I thought that if I was out and became anxious, I would drink to relax and wouldn't be able to stop myself from drinking too much. I reduced the amount of alcohol I drank when I was alone. Instead of binging by myself, I drank only one beer a night a few times per week. Doctors can argue about this all day long, but I think that having a glass or two of wine or beer every night with dinner is fine. Anyone who's spent time in Europe knows that it's simply a way of life there and has been for centuries. The key is to drink moderately.

Lesson #6: Get some freakin' Zen!

"All men's miseries derive from not being able to sit in a quiet room alone."

BLAISE PASCAL
(World-renowned scientist and mathematician who abandoned his scientific work and devoted his life to philosophy and theology after a brush with death)

Are you afraid of silence? When was the last time you turned off the television, the cell phone, pushed the magazines aside, and just sat quietly alone with yourself? In today's Western society, this isn't something we seem to like to do. However, becoming comfortable with silence and mastering sitting still are important keys to overcoming fears in your life.

I used to be scared of silence and didn't want to spend any time alone with my thoughts. I relied on distractions, most often television and music. Once I learned the importance and incredible benefits of learning how to meditate and slow things down, my life really changed. Sitting quietly and meditating made a tremendous difference and helped me finally conquer my panic attacks.

Lesson #7: Get reconnected.

Sometimes you just feel out of balance. You know that you've strayed too far from the path you'd like to be on. It's time to get reconnected.

What makes you feel good? Maybe it's visiting and catching up with family or friends. Or maybe getting back on a bicycle and riding around like you used to, or practicing photography, or going fishing or out on hikes into nature. Whatever it is for you, get back into it!

Look, we're all busy, so that's not an excuse. No one *has* time. Instead, we have to *make* time for what's important. And I can't think of anything more important than feeling good.

Lesson #8: Take breaks.

It is easy to get caught up in our daily tasks. Now and then, you need to step away.

We all need breaks. In many cultures, mealtime is sacred and is to be spent with friends and loved ones. Grabbing takeout and eating at your desk (or worse, while driving your car) is not a lunch break!

Here is something I observed while living in Europe, and I have applied it to my life. No matter how crazy and busy things were in the office, my European colleagues *always* took a long lunch break followed by a walk outside. They also took at least two twenty-minute (or longer) coffee breaks every day.

Work will always be there, and your health has to come first. Your mind is the engine that powers your life, and if you keep stomping on the accelerator without letting up, your engine is going to blow. So take your foot off the gas pedal and chill out!

Make taking breaks a priority and part of your every day. A coffee break is more than filling up your cup with java and going straight back to your desk. Take fifteen minutes or more to really step away from it all.

"But I'm too busy—I have too much to do!" Everyone is busy, that's not an excuse. Besides, after you return to work after taking a break, you'll find you're thinking far more clearly and efficiently.

Lesson #9: Think beyond anxiety.

> *"What man actually needs is not a tensionless state but rather the striving and struggling for a worthwhile goal, a freely chosen task."*
>
> Viktor E. Frankl
> (survived more than two years of imprisonment in concentration camps during World War II, author of *Man's Search for Meaning*)

When we don't have a greater goal or purpose for ourselves in mind, our bored and uninspired minds tend to create their own problems. It gives us something to do.

One reason people get stuck with anxiety is that they focus on it constantly. They trade in their dreams for worry. Forget anxiety for a minute, and try to remember what you actually want in life, not what you fear.

Want to see the pyramids in Egypt? Dream of owning a vineyard in Tuscany? Always wanted to become a stand-up comedian? All these things are still possible, don't forget that.

> *"The greater danger for most of us lies not in setting our aim too high and falling short, but in setting our aim too low, and achieving our mark."*
>
> MICHELANGELO
> (Renaissance sculptor, architect, poet, and artist most famous for his masterpiece: the Sistine Chapel in Rome)

Don't give anxiety all of your attention. Instead, dream of being, doing, and having whatever you want.

EXAMINING YOUR THOUGHTS

How do you think? That may seem like a strange question to you, but it's one to consider. Many factors contribute to putting one in an anxious state. The predominant cause may be faulty thinking.

Unfortunately, many of us do think in flawed ways, *especially* anxiety sufferers. In this section the most common types of flawed thinking are discussed. Also, I'll give examples of how I fell into each trap, and explain what you can do to escape these pitfalls.

*"Just as the gardener cultivates his plot, keeping it
free from weeds, and growing the flowers and fruits
which he requires, so may a man tend the garden of his
mind, weeding out all the wrong, useless, and impure
thoughts, and cultivating towards perfection the flowers
and fruits of right, useful, and pure thoughts."*

James Allen, *As a Man Thinketh*
(British philosopher and author who, at age 38, quit his industrial job to pursue
writing and philosophy)

The what-if virus

What if I write this book and everyone who knows me finds out
these horrible secrets and thinks I'm crazy? What if they no longer
want to be my friends? If my co-workers found out, would I lose
my job?

Do these sound familiar? Thoughts like these poisoned my mind
for years. Some were so frightening that I no longer trusted myself
and feared what I might be capable of. Although I've never been a
violent person, having panic attacks made me feel as if I could no
longer control myself. Was I actually capable of following through
with these extreme thoughts?

In talking with others who have suffered from anxiety, it seems
many of us share the same scary and somewhat silly worrisome
thoughts. I've listed some below. Can you relate to these?

Examples of irrational what-if thoughts

Setting: Office meeting in a conference room
What if...

- I can't take the anxiety and anticipation of speaking before it's my turn, and I have to run out of the conference room?
- I stand up and scream and call my boss a #%!%@# idiot?
- I can't speak when it's my turn and just sit there, unable to talk?
- I am so nervous that everyone in the room can see how nervous I am?
- I just pass out cold when it's my turn to speak?

Setting: Crowded train/ski gondola/elevator
What if...

- I have a panic attack and have to get out but can't and everyone just watches in horror?
- I stand up, scream obscenities, and try to pry open the doors?

Setting: On a plane
What if...

- I freak out and try to break a window or open the door?
- I physically struggle with a flight attendant or another passenger for no reason?
- I try to break into the cockpit to force the pilot to land so I can get out of the plane?

Setting: In a hotel room on a high floor
What if...

- I run out and jump off the balcony?
- I grab stuff from the room and start throwing it out the window?

Setting: Driving a car
What if. . .

- I suddenly yank the wheel and head into an embankment or off a cliff?
- I flip out and run over pedestrians?
- I scream uncontrollably and drive head-on toward oncoming traffic?
- I speed and a cop tries to pull me over and I lead him on a high-speed car chase, cause a horrible crash, and end up in prison for the rest of my life?

Setting: Seated in a barber's or dentist's chair
What if. . .

- I have to get up out of the chair and just run out in panic with the work half done?

Setting: On a date
What if. . .

- I just freak out and have to leave right in the middle of dinner?
- I get so nervous that I can't handle myself when I'm alone with an attractive woman?

If you're suffering from extreme social anxiety and panic attacks, these what-ifs may sound familiar.

So what are these crazy what-if thoughts all about? Why are you obsessing over these things?

People like to be in control, or at least feel like they are, whether it's driving a car or deciding what food to order. When panic comes, you don't know what you can believe about anything, including yourself. Something you took for granted your whole life, the fact that you have control over your own body and actions, has seemingly been taken away from you. If you did have control, you wouldn't worry about these things, right?

Through my own experience, I've found that you're probably not going to act out any of these crazy thoughts. The worst that's going to happen when these thoughts are racing through your mind is that your anxiety levels will increase and you may trigger a panic attack. That's it.

You are in control of every thought that enters your mind; you just may not believe it yet. By the end of this book, I hope you will.

Because these thoughts often will come to you while you are in an anxious situation, you must deal with them as they arise. Later in this book, I will discuss techniques for getting yourself through such circumstances.

A good way to combat harmful what-if thoughts is to examine them when you are calm and thinking clearly. Take each one of your scary what-ifs and analyze it. Ask yourself:

* In the past, have I ever acted out this crazy thought in the same situation?

* What are the actual chances that I would act out so crazily? Calculate it. If you've been on a train 2,000 times in your life, but you had a panic attack once, that's 1/2,000 or just 0.0005% of the time. How's that for some perspective?

* Realize statistically how rare such a reaction is, and you'll see for yourself how silly worrying about it is. This is like worrying about getting struck by lightning.

All or nothing

In this case, you can see only one possibility or outcome—the absolute worst one imaginable. Another term for this type of thinking is called *catastrophization*.

You don't even entertain the idea that things might go well enough, just not perfectly or horrendously bad. In your mind, you visualize only perfection or complete failure.

Almost always, your experience will be somewhere in the middle. You won't freak out and lose control, but you will likely be a bit anxious at first and then eventually settle down. That's it.

Catch yourself when your thoughts are going this way, and quickly recognize that your experience will fall somewhere in the middle and that you'll be just fine. Understand that it's okay to be anxious, and that being anxious doesn't mean you're going to lose control. Like any extreme emotion, it will eventually pass and you will calm down.

False associations

I was reading a German book on the el when my first panic attack in Chicago occurred. After I fled the train in panic, I remember thinking, "I'll never read a German book again!"

Then I switched to taking the bus to work. I remember vowing not to take any German books with me. I didn't want reading a book to conjure up any memories of that panic attack on the el.

Reflecting back now with a rational perspective, I know the book itself had nothing to do with my panic attack. I linked the book, however, with the bad experience on the train, and thus avoided it. I had created a false association so strong that anytime I even looked at one of my German books at home, my first thoughts were about the panic attack.

Fortunately, our brains are very powerful. We have the ability to examine the validity of our beliefs and challenge and change them as we choose.

The best way to do this is to prove your false associations wrong and create new healthy ones. Once you overcome your fear of something by continually facing it, you can learn to link pleasure or happiness to that experience instead of fear and dread. Just remember: such change takes time.

What's your disposition?

The first time you notice something, anything that enters your field of vision or pops into your head, what is your initial reaction to it? When you see an attractive or very successful person, do you busy yourself with trying to find their flaws? When you think about something you've always wanted, do all of the reasons you'll never obtain it follow?

If you're thinking like this, it's as if you're walking around wearing a pair of darkly tinted glasses. Everything you see is shaded with a negative and hopeless outlook. Recognize that this is not healthy! This pessimistic view of the world is likely a product of the depression and frustration that accompany anxiety.

A good way to overcome this is to catch yourself in the act. Make it a point to be conscious of what your thoughts are throughout the day. If they seem to be negatively skewed, acknowledge this immediately and replace them with positive or even neutral thoughts.

I've found the easiest way to minimize negative thoughts is by feeling gratitude. For example, if I'm annoyed with a co-worker, I try to focus on being thankful for having a good job and living in an abundant Western society. If I'm walking down the street and becoming impatient with crowds of tourists, I try to think about how lucky I am to live in a place people want to visit.

Start out small. See if you can go five minutes without falling into a negative thinking pattern. Gradually increase how long you are mindful of your thoughts until it becomes a part of your routine. If you keep at it, this can translate into a very healthy and beneficial lifestyle change. Eliminate some of the negativity from your life, and you'll be surprised at how it positively affects your mood and outlook.

Predicting the future

Is there something you wish you could do but, due to fear, you don't dare attempt it? Why? Because you know you can't do it? How do you know? If you're truly able to predict the future, wouldn't it be a better use of time to focus on next week's winning lottery numbers?

No one can predict the future. However, if you tell yourself you can't do something, then you are 100 percent correct. Anything that you feel and believe strongly, your subconscious mind goes to work to make it a reality.

Luckily, just the opposite is also true. When you tell yourself you *can* do something, you absolutely can. You activate all of your mental and physical resources to make it a reality. This is what you want to do.

Again, it's important to catch yourself in the act. Be mindful of saying things such as "Oh, I could never do that" or "I'll never achieve that." Quickly restate out loud, "If I really want to do that or achieve that goal, I know I can." This is the beginning of training your mind to think in other, more positive ways and opens the possibility of success.

The "Should" game

"I shouldn't feel anxious or nervous in this situation. I should be stronger and more relaxed. I should be able to do this, so why can't I?"

If this is what you think, clean all that "should" off of you! When you think this way, all you are doing is putting more pressure on yourself and focusing your attention on things you don't like. When you say the word *should*, you create an image or template that you believe is the way things are supposed to be. When you don't fit into this mold, you're going to depress and frustrate yourself further.

The next time you catch yourself saying you "should" be or act a certain way, stop right there. Understand that it's okay if you don't meet such ridiculous expectations. After all, who said such standards were correct or even possible? I highly recommend trying to eliminate the word *should* from your vocabulary.

Emotional logic

When you're not feeling well, what kind of a mood are you in? You may feel weak, depressed, and anxious. In such a state, your view of the world is misaligned. Because you feel so poorly, you think poorly. You talk yourself out of taking on challenges, because you can't fathom how you could possibly accomplish them. This triggers a cycle of depression and maladaptive thinking that can be difficult to overcome.

The trick is to understand that your thoughts control your feelings. Just because you may feel bad, don't interpret that to mean you can't do something or that you are helpless or weak. **Think logically with your mind instead of illogically with your emotions.** Recognize that most of the negative emotions you feel due to your anxiety are useless clutter and have no basis in reality.

"Truth is incontrovertible. Ignorance may attack it and malice may deride it, but in the end, there it is."

SIR WINSTON CHURCHILL
(Prime Minster of the United Kingdom during World War II, famous for his heroic leadership and clever quotes)

The rational truth is within your mind, but it's difficult to find when you are distracted by your emotions. Try to see past your anxious thoughts and worries and think about things logically. When you do, you will begin to realize what a waste of time and energy worrying can be. Your irrational emotions are simply diverting your attention from the truth. Don't let them!

THE POWER OF BELIEFS

"Whether you think you can or you think you can't, either way, you are right."

HENRY FORD
(founder of Ford Motor Company and father of the modern assembly line)

As I learned more about Buddhism, read more self-help books, and began to practice the principles both teach, one underlying point revealed itself. **Your world, no matter how wonderful or awful it is, is shaped by your thoughts. You create your own reality, and it's your decision whether to make it a wonderful or dreadful place.**

Beliefs are powerful. Problems arise when we create and focus upon negative and limiting beliefs. We may use past experiences as proof that things won't work out for us, or that we'll never be happy. Constantly thinking like this only serves to reinforce and strengthen the negative belief.

Maybe a young man has a crush on a cute girl. After months, he finally musters up the courage to ask her out on a date, but she says that she's not interested, and that she already has a boyfriend. The man feels rejected and deflated, and if he's not thinking rationally, he can get himself into some real trouble mentally. He may begin to assume that any girl he's attracted to must already have a boyfriend. Maybe they claim they do to avoid going out with him. Therefore, it's no use even trying to ask them out. See how limiting and untrue this thinking can be?

When many people think about a difficult and intimidating task, they claim that they could never do it. Well, guess what? They're right. They've already eliminated the possibility of succeeding because they've told themselves they can't do it. They probably won't even attempt it.

After I had a panic attack while waiting to introduce myself to a roomful of colleagues, I developed a belief that I was unable to speak in public. Did I believe this was true? Absolutely! I had proof. I had experienced a panic attack in front of a group of people and was barely able to speak. For years, that was my evidence that I was incapable of public speaking. It didn't matter that I had previously spoken in public countless other times. This single experience had produced a panic attack, so I now believed 100 percent that I couldn't do it.

The same thing happened when I had a panic attack while riding the el in Chicago. After that, I was unable to ride any crowded trains, for I believed if I did I would have another panic attack. Again, I had proof.

The longer you believe something, the stronger your convictions become. You reinforce them with your thoughts, over and over again. Your mind doesn't distinguish whether these beliefs are negative or positive—all it knows is what you keep feeding it. Your mind responds accordingly, and subconsciously does all it can to make your beliefs reality.

This is what I'm trying to drive home in this section. Whatever you believe in and think about with strong emotion will eventually become your reality. What will it be for you? Will it be success and triumph or failure and defeat? The choice is yours. You, and you alone, control your beliefs.

A great example of this is what is known as the placebo effect. A placebo may be used in clinical studies when determining the effectiveness of new medications. Some of the patients will be given the new medication, and the others will be given what they believe is the real medication, but it's actually a sugar pill (the placebo). The results can be astounding. Many people heal themselves even though they are taking the placebo.

How can this be? Because the patient believes the pill is helping to cure him, his mindset and attitude change. The patient expects to be healed. This aligns with the principles of "mind-body medicine" described by famous medical doctor and writer Deepak Chopra (reference: http://en.wikipedia.org/wiki/Deepak_Chopra).

Simply opening your mind to the possibility of healing and remaining in a relaxed and resourceful state of mind, your body can perform miracles. This is the power of positive beliefs in action.

ELIMINATING YOUR HARMFUL BELIEFS

Most of us have empowered or developed negative beliefs. When you've identified some of your harmful and limiting beliefs, how do you change them? Unfortunately, it's not a matter of simply deciding that you won't believe them any longer. You've probably become too attached to them. The only way to eliminate them is to directly challenge their validity. You are going to have to face that which you have been avoiding for weeks, months, maybe even years. These activities may include driving, going to the grocery store, speaking in public, flying, or whatever. The bottom line is that you're going to have to face them.

"FEAR—False Evidence that Appears Real."

AUTHOR UNKNOWN

By facing your fears, you directly challenge the false beliefs you've created in your mind. Something astounding and empowering happens once you do this: You start to think, "Wow, if I can do this, I can do anything! What other fears do I have that are also false?"

No matter how bad off you think you are, you are capable of facing your very worst fear right now. The power is already inside of you, begging to be unleashed.

Think from the end

Too often we get caught up in worrying about the journey instead of the destination. We talk ourselves out of the possibility of reaching what we desire. We can't conceive of how we'd possibly make it through the many obstacles that are sure to arise along the way, so we don't even try.

Say you've always wanted to have your own business, but you tell yourself it will never happen because you don't know anything about incorporating, tax laws, accounting, and other important aspects of business. So, you never even attempt it, because you can't envision how you'll ever make it. The trick is to focus on achieving the end result and to not get hung up on the difficulty of the journey in between.

Dwell on reaching that goal and how wonderful it will feel to do so. Every single time doubt arises, immediately catch it. Then, replace it with the exciting thought of reaching your goal and feeling proud.

Performance anxiety

This type of anxiety stems from a fear of disapproval or rejection by your peers or an audience and can take many forms. At the root, they can be traced back to a poor self-image and low self-confidence.

Almost everyone experiences performance anxiety to some extent. The following are some examples of how performance anxiety affected me. You'll probably relate to a few of these.

Public speaking
I've heard many times that most people are more afraid of public speaking than death. Comedian Jerry Seinfeld has joked about this, saying that most people at a funeral would rather to be in the casket than give the eulogy! For most of my adult life, I certainly felt this way.

When I was a small child, I loved the spotlight and being up in front of my peers. But by the time I got to high school, something happened. I became so worried and concerned with fitting in and not embarrassing myself that I began to really dread public speaking. Dread turned into fear, which grew and grew.

Baseball: Swing away!

Like most American boys, I loved baseball and played for many years. When playing for fun among my friends, I was a good player and loved it. Playing in formal games though, scared the hell out of me. In fourth grade, I was too timid to even swing the bat! I was terrified of swinging and missing and looking foolish in front of everyone.

One day, one of the other parents realized what I was feeling and really fired me up. She said "Just swing! It doesn't matter if you hit it or not, just swing!" So I did. Guess what? I hit the ball on the first try!

This set off a chain of positive events. My self-confidence went through the roof, and I finally felt like a valued member of the team. I practiced and became a very good hitter. Then I couldn't wait to get up to bat and have my chance to swing away. For the next two seasons, I even tried out for and played in a competitive league where the opposition was much tougher. Had I never taken that first swing that fateful day in fourth grade, I would not have made it that far.

> *"If you do the best you can, you will find, nine times out of ten, that you have done as well as or better than anyone else."*
>
> WILLIAM FEATHER, (American author and publisher)

Golf: Teeing off

Because I hadn't had any exposure to it, I didn't pick up golf until my freshman year of high school. I fell in love with it immediately. I landed a job at a driving range near my parents' house so I could practice for free and worked hard to improve my game. Now, what does this have to do with performance anxiety?

Well, picture this: You're waiting for your turn to tee off on the first hole of a high school golf tournament. Surrounding this first tee are golfers from other schools and their coaches, tournament officials, and parents of some of the golfers. When you tee off, the crowd, no matter how large, is dead quiet and all eyes are on you. Talk about pressure! If this isn't one of the ultimate tests of performance anxiety, I don't know what is.

As much as I practiced and believed in my abilities as a golfer, the very thought of this first tee scenario constantly haunted me. The recommended way to improve your score is to focus most of your time practicing shots from 100 yards and closer to the hole. This includes putting, chipping, pitching, and all sorts of finesse shots that have nothing to do with hitting that drive off of the first tee in front of everyone.

But to me, the most important thing wasn't to post a great score at a tournament. I just didn't want to be embarrassed! I didn't want to look like a fool on the first tee in front of everyone. I was so concerned about *appearing* to be a good golfer on the first tee and impressing people with my first shot that I didn't care much about my overall score. Good thing my golf coach didn't know this!

It sounds ridiculous now, but I was far less ashamed of having a bad score posted up on the scoreboard than I would have been if I completely choked on one shot with everyone watching. I later recognized this as flawed thinking.

Did reading these stories about my anxieties conjure up any similar memories for you?

As I reflect upon my early life (I'm 30 as I'm writing this), I can easily spot many situations and reactions that were yellow warning lights that I've had performance anxiety my entire life. My beliefs about myself and the importance I placed on gaining approval from others brought my anxieties about. I have had to overcome this myself.

Not all anxiety is bad. Anytime you're preparing to perform in some way, a little nervous energy helps you to focus. When you let your worries and anticipatory anxiety become debilitating, though, you need to think about making some changes.

The Piano: Playing for the family

I've always admired musicians such as Billy Joel and Elton John. In college, I wanted to learn to play the piano. I took a few courses in the limited free time I had, and though I didn't learn to read music, I could play a few songs from memory.

One Easter celebration at my uncle's house, I went to the living room by myself to play the piano. Soon, my relatives were pouring into the room to hear me play.

I put a ton of pressure on myself to play the songs correctly. Before I knew it, my hands were shaking so badly that I could hardly hit the correct keys. My heart was pounding. What was happening?

What I took away from that afternoon's experience was mostly confusion. This was before panic attacks became part of my life, and I didn't know much about anxiety. Thus, I just shrugged it off as stage fright. Why was I so nervous playing a piano in front of my loving and supportive family? I would understand why later.

PHYSICAL SYMPTOMS OF PANIC AND ANXIETY

Anxiety wreaks havoc on the body. The following are some of the physical symptoms you may experience when under extreme stress and worry.

Out-of-body feeling
Severe bouts of anxiety may cause you a weird, almost spacey, out-of-body feeling. I experienced this on and off for years. It seemed I was watching my life, not actually living it.

If you experience this, view it as your mind's way of checking out for a while. If you are putting yourself through tremendous stress with constant worrying, this may happen. Realize that while your mind and body are taking a short vacation, you can come along for the trip. Know that these feelings won't hurt you, and their power over you disappears. Accepting symptoms that frighten you will help you to overcome and stop reacting to them.

On some occasions, especially while speaking in public, I still encounter this feeling. If I'm about to give a prepared speech, as I sit, waiting to be introduced to the crowd, my anxiety levels rise. Despite having to stand up and give a speech while feeling spacey, often as soon as I begin to speak the feelings of anxiety rapidly disappear. So now when I am feeling this way, I don't let it scare me. Instead I simply observe the feelings and know I don't have to react to them or become frightened.

Tension headaches
Another anxiety-related symptom I've had is tension headaches.

Besides the panic attacks themselves, this was one of the first symptoms I noticed and wanted to treat.

So what do these feel like? Have you ever gone to a factory and put your head into a large hydraulic press that's used to crush steel? Me neither, but I imagine it's the same feeling.

Sometimes it's a constant ache, while other times my whole head throbs. The pain may come and go throughout the day, and it may stick around off and on for months.

I had all sorts of tests done, including an MRI (magnetic resonance image). During this test, you are slid into a claustrophobic tube like a torpedo and told to lie still for twenty minutes—lots of fun for a panic sufferer! To my surprise, the doctors found nothing physically wrong with me. But the pain continued and even intensified, lasting for three or four months.

As with other symptoms, these headaches and feelings do eventually go away. I viewed them as another warning sign from my body that I was in the red zone. My engine was about to blow, and I needed to make some serious changes.

Go to a doctor and get examined to make sure you're in good health. If you're experiencing the same symptoms, these may be tension headaches.

Eye twitches

Years ago, during an especially busy and stressful period in college, I worked about thirty hours per week at a restaurant, had a full load of engineering courses, and a girlfriend. Stretched among these activities I had almost no downtime. Out of nowhere, my eye started twitching involuntarily. Sometimes it lasted for hours at a time, and happened for many months. Finally, when summer arrived and my schedule eased up, it went away.

I asked my regular doctor about the eye twitches. He said they are common for those experiencing a lot of stress and lack of sleep. He mentioned that many medical students experience this while overloaded with coursework and barely sleeping.

When I first started having panic attacks, this symptom reappeared. If you experience it, anxiety may be the cause. Once you reduce your anxiety levels, many minor symptoms such as this disappear.

Upset stomach

Ever hear the term *nervous stomach*? During my years of struggling with anxiety, this was a part of my daily life. I even went to the doctor and got on medication, as the doctor believed I had irritable bowel syndrome. However, now that I've gotten past my anxiety problems, my stomach rarely bothers me.

Again, I recommend you go to a doctor and get examined, but you may find as I did that once you get a handle on your anxiety, this symptom may disappear.

RETOOLING YOUR THINKING

When anxiety ruled my life, very often I would call in sick to avoid going to work. I was afraid of so many social situations that I ran and hid from them. This only made me feel worse about myself and my situation. Through avoidance, I took power away from myself and gave it to my fears.

Although I wasn't physically ill, I told myself I deserved to feel sick because I was faking it. Most of the time, my body responded accordingly and I *would* feel awful. By the end of the day, I'd feel ill and completely drained of energy both mentally and physically.

How could this be? What you need to understand is that thoughts really are things, and that your reality is created within your mind. If you have a poor self-image and tell yourself you deserve to feel bad and unmotivated, that's exactly what happens.

Say you wake up in a bad mood, and you just don't feel well. As you dwell on not feeling well, you start to attract more negative feelings and thoughts until you physically feel even worse. Because you have put yourself in a negative state, you begin to notice the negative aspects of everything around you. Little things irritate you, you have a frown on your face, and the world seems to be out to get you.

Let's say this is your experience one day, and then out of nowhere someone comes up to you and hands you a check for a million dollars. What happens to your mindset? Immediately you'll snap out of this negative and depressed state you've been in and feel nothing but joy, gratitude, and excitement.

The trick is that you don't need a million-dollar check to change your state of mind (although it wouldn't hurt!). You already possess the power to change and shape your thoughts, which determine your level of overall happiness or unhappiness. Once you learn to master your thoughts, you will understand that no external influences can change your mood or state, for **it is your choice how you interpret the world within your mind.**

MEDITATION:
IT'S NOT JUST FOR MONKS!

"When you have attained peace of mind, your mind will automatically reject every thought and mental reaction that is not beneficial to your welfare. But before you graduate into this desirable command of your mind, you will find it necessary to voluntarily throw off all negative mental influences that you do not wish to become a part of your character. 'Throwing off' consists of transmuting negative thoughts into positive thoughts. This is done by simply switching your mind away from unpleasant thoughts and training it on thoughts that are pleasant."

NAPOLEON HILL
(author of the groundbreaking self-improvement book *Think and Grow Rich*)

Meditation. For me, that word used to conjure up images of a wise, gray-haired monk in the middle of a cave in Tibet contorted into some crazy yoga position. Now that I have learned about it and practice it often, I know that meditation is a wonderfully therapeutic endeavor that can benefit anyone.

Why should I meditate?

If you're like many people in our fast-paced Western society, you don't know how to slow down. All day long, countless thoughts fly in and out of your mind. If you stop and monitor these thoughts, you'll find that some of them are pretty useless, or at least not beneficial to you. Even worse—some of us high-anxiety types *love* to worry about things and picture worst-case scenarios.

As we go through our daily routines, more and more of these thoughts arise and build up in our minds. What's the result? More stress, more anger, more frustration, and, of course, more anxiety.

Meditation is the best way I've found to unclog and quiet your mind. **By spending time alone with your thoughts, you learn that you are in control of them and your reactions to them.** As you progress, focusing your attention on positive thoughts and feelings becomes easier. In turn, negative thoughts and feelings drop away.

If you're suffering from severe anxiety, however, meditation can be terrifying as you are likely very afraid of the scary thoughts that plague your mind. This is exactly why meditation will help you, because it gives you a chance to cleanse your mind and find peace.

So how do you meditate? Do you need to buy an audiotape that will guide you through it? If you want to do that, go ahead, but I've found the best results come with complete silence.

How I meditate

I've found the best time of the day to meditate is first thing in the morning. I awake in a relaxed state and my mind is clear and fresh. Within fifteen minutes of waking up, I go to a quiet place and put in earplugs to block out any distractions. I usually begin by spending a few minutes reading something inspirational—maybe some passages from a favorite self-help book or a list I've made of all that I want to accomplish, experience, and manifest in my life. Sometimes I look at photos of wonderful trips I've taken or photos of places I'd love to see. The key is to find something that gets your emotions and thoughts moving in a positive and hopeful direction. With these motivating thoughts and images fresh in my head, I close my eyes and focus my attention on the simple in and out of my breath. I observe the thoughts in my mind and steer them toward pleasant thoughts and visions. If something unpleasant pops into my head, I divert my attention away from it and back towards pleasing thoughts.

I've found that I can reach a very relaxed and peaceful state after twenty minutes or so. I try to allot thirty minutes of meditation per session, but sometimes it just feels so good that I open my eyes and discover an hour has passed. Meditating for a few minutes will help, but you may have a more meaningful experience if you allow your mind more time to grow quiet. (Believe me, I know how cheesy that sounds. Now that I have experienced firsthand the benefits of meditation, I embrace my cheesiness!)

Learning to meditate

When you first attempt meditation you will notice many different thoughts racing at you from every direction. This is normal. Your mind isn't used to being still, so initially it will resist. Just remember that you are in control, and that you dictate what thoughts you have. Observe the thoughts that race toward you, but do not react to them. Simply observe them and watch them fall away and lose their strength.

After a few minutes, you will notice that you are becoming calm and that fewer thoughts are coming at you. You are beginning to tap into the magic of meditation: time spent in complete stillness. In this state, you become aware that you are in charge of your thoughts, and you are free to visualize anything.

When I reach this state, I concentrate on whatever inspirational materials I looked at just before beginning my mediation. I focus on what I want to experience and manifest in my life, and I visualize in great detail these things happening. If I find my thoughts turning negative, I don't react strongly. Instead, I gently steer them back toward what I want.

At first, meditating for only a few minutes will seem difficult, but as you stick with it and become accustomed to being alone with your thoughts, time may seem to fly by.

Meditation tips for beginners:

1) **Stay with it.** You may become anxious the first few times you attempt to meditate. Think of meditation as a way of cleansing your mind of bad thoughts and negative energy. If you haven't spent much time in quiet thought, your mind has a lot of garbage to clear out. Just know that eventually your mind will become quiet. If you do become anxious, stay in the experience! Don't react, get up, or open your eyes. Stay in the moment, and know that it will pass. You will become stronger and more relaxed by enduring it.

   Many people, including myself, find it easier at first to meditate with guided meditation. This often consists of an instructional audio program paired with soothing music and sounds to help you relax. I found these programs helpful when I was panic-stricken, but I now prefer to meditate in pure silence or to soothing music or ambient sounds (think waterfalls). For a list of recommended meditation programs visit: **http://www.alifelessanxious.com/**

2) **Focus on positive desires.** If you've been having anxiety problems, it's normal to continually visualize scary and unpleasant situations. This is not going to help you, so it's up to you to steer your thoughts in alternative directions.

Focus your energy on visualizing what you want to experience, people you want to meet, and places you want to travel. Pay attention to the most minute details of the experience you desire—how the food tastes, the smells in the air, the sounds of waves crashing on the shore, and the feeling of sand between your toes. This attention to detail makes the experience more vivid and helps you to manifest it in your life.

3) **Start small.** Set a goal of ten minutes the first few times you meditate. As you continue along, you'll notice how good meditating makes you feel. Accordingly, the length of time you spend in meditation will increase. You may be busy, but you can still set aside thirty minutes in the morning and evening for meditation.

    At first, it may seem like a chore, but as the benefits of this practice reveal themselves to you, you'll realize how important it is to make time for it. Once you have finished a session, allow a few minutes to slowly come out of your meditation. You will feel so relaxed!

4) **Be opportunistic.** Taking a long flight? Riding a train for hours? Waiting in the doctor's office forever? Seize these opportunities to meditate! Instead of mindlessly thumbing through a magazine, or instinctively turning on your iPod, try closing your eyes and just relaxing.

5) **Try different techniques.** One form of meditation may not suit you, while another is a perfect fit. You'll never know unless you experiment. Try guided meditation. Try meditating in silence. Try meditating to some New Age chant music while balancing on your head. Whatever makes you feel best, go with it.

6) **Practice daily.** Maintaining a quiet, peaceful mind requires regular housekeeping. By meditating daily, you minimize the

amount of stress, tension, and negativity that can build up in your mind. Practicing often also makes reaching a deep state of relaxation much easier.

SHIFT YOUR PERSPECTIVE

Having the proper perspective can do wonders for your attitude and overall well-being. If you look at the problems you've had with anxiety and say, "Why me?" or "What did I do to deserve this?" you're way off target. Thinking like this is only going to frustrate you.

> *"Struggle is a clever device through which Nature compels humanity to develop, expand and progress. It is either an ordeal or a magnificent experience, depending on one's attitude toward it. Success is impossible—unthinkable even—without it."*
>
> NAPOLEON HILL
> (author of the groundbreaking self-improvement book *Think and Grow Rich*)

One of the most powerful things you can do when thinking about the problems you have in your life is to shift your perspective. Instead of dwelling on the problem and its negative effects on you, ask yourself the following questions:

* What can I learn from this?
* What are the positives I can draw from this experience?
* How can I use these problems to improve my life?

When your thinking shifts to thoughts such as these instead of thoughts of self-pity or depression, you open yourself to a whole new world of possibilities. A solution becomes possible. Instead of feeling hopeless, you begin to believe that there is hope after all. This opens your inner door and allows more good feelings to pour in.

> *"The mind can make a heaven out of hell or a hell out of heaven."*
>
> JOHN MILTON
> (17th-century English poet famous for his epic work *Paradise Lost*)

It's like driving a car. . .

You have likely developed anxiety problems because you've been stuck in a negative thinking rut for some time. Getting out of that rut is not as difficult as you may think. It really is a lot like driving a car.

Let's say you're driving to a place called Happiness, where anything you desire, you can have. All you have to do is follow the road signs along the way, and eventually you will reach this magical destination. Unfortunately, you keep taking exits marked Freak-out-over-nothing Avenue, Self-sabotage Lane, and Constant Worry Boulevard. In extreme cases, you decide to jerk the wheel through the guardrail and plummet into dreaded Panic Attack Valley.

Don't despair. Even if you've been wandering around lost in Panic Attack Valley for years, you can always find your way back to the Road to Happiness. Many people have, including me.

Your mind, like a car, does not steer itself. You guide your thoughts just as you turn a steering wheel. Where you direct them is up to you. Recognizing that you are deciding to become anxious and panicky is a major step. Once you grasp this, you are ready to use this awareness to your advantage.

Be honest and ask yourself right now: What is constantly on your mind? Is your answer fear and paranoia? For years, I would have given this answer. I doubt I ever went more than an hour or two (except when I was asleep!) when I wasn't thinking about something I feared.

I no longer thought about the good things in life. I forgot about my wonderful dreams and ambitions. I fed panic my undivided attention, so guess what happened to my hopes and dreams? I forgot all about them. If I thought about something else, could it also become my world?

YES! I am telling you right now, 1,000 percent yes yes yes! Get back to your life and do what you want to do with it. I know you may be feeling low, depressed, frustrated, and overwhelmed by panic and anxiety, but I'm guessing you haven't always been like this.

Close your eyes and take yourself back to a wonderful time in your life. Remember the sights, the sounds, the feelings, things you touched and held, people you spoke to and embraced. Try to recall the smallest details of the experience.

You can conjure up those feelings again by visualizing and remembering the experience. Remember how you stood, how you walked, how you sat. Remember the food you ate, the hugs, the kisses, the recognition you received from others, the praise, the sweet rewards of success.

Is this already making you feel better? What is to prevent you from feeling this good at any time? Nothing! You see, just by remembering or picturing pleasant experiences, we can put ourselves into a positive and resourceful state. Whatever is going on in your life, if you are thinking about positive and inspirational thoughts, they fill your mind and become your reality.

What would you do if you knew there was no chance you would fail? Visualize these things. Picture them. Feel them. Just like your pleasant memory exercise, you will begin to get those great feelings. You will become inspired.

Before you go to bed for the night, repeat this visualization exercise. Picture what you want in your life. Take a step back from focusing on this tiny part of your life (your anxiety), and look at the big picture. Ever heard the expression, "I couldn't see the forest for the trees"? Essentially, anxiety is just one little tree in your forest. So, take a step back and see the whole forest. Isn't it amazing? Isn't it huge? Doesn't it contain countless trees, as far as you can see in every direction? So why should you give this one little tree all of your attention and forget about the others? Think of all those other trees as your hopes and dreams. Realize how much more powerful and plentiful they are than your fears and worries.

MAKING LIFE CHANGES

Learning to think properly is just the first step, and it works with other lifestyle changes you can make. The following is a summary of the actions described previously that work for me:

* **Slow Down!** Stop walking so fast, driving so fast, eating so fast, pacing nervously when you're waiting, tapping your foot

uncontrollably while sitting at your desk. Just slow down! Do your best to live in the moment and understand that there is no need to rush. Getting yourself in a hurry will make you feel more anxious and flustered. Remember, we're not racing to our graves, so pull up a chair and stay a while.

- **Spend time being quiet and still.** In a sense, this is meditation, but don't let that intimidate you. Spend time each day alone with your thoughts, without distractions. If you're afraid of your thoughts, that's even more reason to get to know them.

- **Focus your thoughts on what you want.** Shift your thoughts to what you want in life. When you shift your attention away from what you don't want, you will find it rapidly fades away.

- **Have gratitude.** Find things every day to appreciate and be grateful for. Recite them out loud or write down a list. This will help you to realize how blessed and lucky you are in so many aspects of your life. You will be in a much better state of mind.

- **Remember your dreams.** Is there something you've always dreamed of doing but haven't yet due to your fear? Remember these aspirations, and learn to focus on them instead of your fears.

Exposures: Pick a fight with your fear

"It is not because things are difficult that we do not dare. It is because we do not dare that they are difficult."

SENECA
(Roman stoic philosopher, statesman, and advisor to Emperor Nero)

Fear has been with all of us for a long time. Perhaps growing up, you were fearful and anxious about going to school. You felt nervous and shy around the other kids and would have preferred to stay at home. However, due to your parents' insistence, not to mention the laws of the United States of America, you *had* to go to school. Like it or not, you were forced into it.

And what happened? No matter how hard it was at first, it eventually became routine. So what became of that fear? You overcame it by continually facing it.

What about fears you have today? Although deep down you may know that you can overcome your fears by facing them, sometimes you decide instead that it's less painful to continually avoid them. In the short term, this avoidance offers temporary relief from any scary situations. In the long term, however, this has a devastating and limiting effect on your life.

> *"It's not what we do that controls us,*
> *it's what we don't do."*

WAYNE DYER
(popular self-help speaker, author of many books including *Your Erroneous Zones* with more than 30 million copies sold)

The only way you're going to overcome the fears that you've developed is to face them down. As you will be making yourself vulnerable or "exposing" yourself to your fears, we'll refer to these experiences as exposures.

Visualization—the simplest way

Most of the time you've spent visualizing may have been wasted on picturing the worst-case scenarios of your what-if thinking. Imagine what it would be like to visualize the best-case scenario. I mean, isn't that also a possibility of what could happen?

Ideally, we are striving for the ability to live in the moment, to rid ourselves of all anticipation of the future and thoughts of the past. Wise people have been saying this for thousands of years, and it's what you'll hear countless modern self-help gurus preach today. **To get there, take a baby step.**

The next time you find yourself thinking about an upcoming event and are feeling anxious, picture the best possible outcome. Here are a few examples:

- If you are anxious about standing in a long line at a grocery store, picture yourself completely relaxed and at peace, standing in line smiling and enjoying small talk with a stranger or watching some children playing in line.

- If you are anxious about having to speak at an upcoming event, picture yourself completely gathered and confident and sitting up straight, projecting a presence of confidence as you breathe calmly while awaiting your turn. Visualize speaking in a firm and confident voice, delighting others with your insights and contributions. Think of some of the great speakers you have seen on television and imagine speaking just as they do.

- If you're anxious about being stuck in a confined space such as an elevator, bus, or plane, picture yourself enjoying the ride and the scenery along the way. Think of how lucky you are to have that time to focus your thoughts inward on whatever you like. If you're not driving but riding in a car, you can totally let go and use this time however you'd like. This can also be a great time to immerse yourself in a good book or a mindlessly entertaining gossip magazine, whatever you want. If you are driving, see being stuck in traffic as another form of freedom. You can turn up your radio to whatever music or self-help audio program you want and be in your own world.

The point in these examples: You create the reality of each situation. If you let your power of imagination and positive thinking take over, you will see the beauty and freedom in what you once considered dreadful situations.

What's your hierarchy?

"Inaction breeds doubt and fear. Action breeds confidence and courage. If you want to conquer fear, do not sit home and think about it. Go out and get busy."

DALE CARNEGIE
(one of the first prominent figures in the field of self-improvement, he taught courses in public speaking, sales, and other interpersonal communications)

What areas of your life cause you great fear and anxiety? Is there a terrifying scenario that you would do absolutely anything to avoid? Are there other activities that you don't avoid doing but still make you feel extremely anxious just thinking about them?

The first step in conquering these fears is to write down these worrisome situations. **In the appendix of this book (as well at the following address:** *http://www.alifelessanxious.com/ hierarchy*) is a worksheet for you to fill out.

Useful tips:

1. DO THIS! This is a vital step in your recovery. For your own benefit, please don't skip over this section of the book and say, "I'll come back to this later." The time to change your life is now. Seize this moment!

2. Be honest with yourself. If something makes you anxious, but you think it's ridiculous that it makes you uncomfortable, write it down. You're not going to share your answers with anyone else.

3. Be sure to add variables for each activity, details that make the activity easier or more difficult. For example, if riding a packed elevator is more difficult than riding an empty elevator, record this.

4. Rank each activity using the following scale:

    5   I would rather die than even attempt it. I can't ever imagine doing this.
    4   I could maybe do this someday, but I avoid it and would be close to fainting if I tried.
    3   I can probably do this but often avoid it, and my stomach is in knots for days just thinking about it.
    2   I do this fairly often, but it still makes me anxious.
    1   I rarely become anxious thinking about this, but sometimes do when I am forced to.

Now review your completed list and ensure that your rankings are correct. This will serve as an outline for your plan of attack in facing your fears.

Now, given your anxious state, you may not want to face some of the exposures listed at the top your anxiety hierarchy. However, I'm sure if you look down at the bottom of your sheet, you will spot some fears you can quickly address and conquer.

The plan of attack

We're going to take small steps to conquer each fear, and each individual victory will move you closer to your goal of freedom. Don't get caught up in how long it takes you to get through your list of fears. What matters is that you keep going.

The goal will be to push yourself to increase the difficulty of exposures on a weekly basis. Start at the bottom of your list. During the first week of your plan, put yourself into that situation as many times as possible. If it's riding an empty elevator instead of taking the stairs, do this every day that week. After a few days, it's time to up the ante. Start waiting for elevators with more and more people, increasing the difficulty for you.

After the first week, it's time to graduate to the next item on your list. As you begin to face situation #2, continue to face situation #1 as often as possible. This is the strategy you will repeat throughout your entire hierarchy. The more you put yourself into these scenarios, the easier they become. Once you start making a dent in your list, don't be surprised if the initial situations you faced cause you no anxiety at all. This is what we're shooting for.

Even after you've made it through your entire list of fears, some of the situations may still make you anxious. This is okay. It's unrealistic to expect all of your anxieties to disappear completely. Rather, what you prove to yourself by facing these fears is that you can do anything, despite being anxious.

Relapses happen. How they affect you, however, is completely up to you. Maybe you make it halfway through your list and have a mild panic attack while facing a situation. Don't overreact and become unraveled. **Remember that progress can take time**. Step back down in your hierarchy to an easier situation to regain your confidence. Then push yourself to face that situation again.

This has much to do with your attitude and overall outlook on life. For example, if a depressed person is playing in a baseball game and strikes out the first time at bat, this might devastate him. He might go back to the dugout with his head hung low, staring at the ground and convinced that he is doomed to fail every time he bats. After one attempt, he has colored his future efforts with failure. He doesn't even want to get up to bat any more. He automatically expects that he will fail and strike out again.

Now consider an optimist placed in the same situation. He strikes out and heads back to the dugout with his head held high. He walks confidently and shrugs his shoulders, because it's no big deal. He thinks to himself, "The pitcher got the best of me this time, but wait until next time!" He hasn't let this one negative outcome poison his outlook or attitude. Instead, he is determined to continue trying until he succeeds.

Success in most cases is simply a matter of not giving up.

"Let me tell you the secret that has led me to my goal. My strength lies solely in my tenacity."

LOUIS PASTEUR
(French chemist who created the first vaccine for rabies and invented the process of pasteurization)

"If I find 10,000 ways something won't work, I haven't failed. I am not discouraged, because every wrong attempt discarded is often a step forward. . . ."

THOMAS EDISON
(American inventor and avatar, holder of more than 1,000 U.S. patents [talk about a creative and determined mind])

What a dramatic example of perseverance. Thomas Edison had more than 10,000 failures in his designs before he created the working light bulb that we still use to this very day. Imagine that! Attempting something 10,000 times and still coming back for more, ever confident that you will reach the solution.

In contrast, how many times have you given up after only one or two failed attempts? Imagine what you would be capable of if you kept going until you reached your goal.

"Great works are performed not by strength, but perseverance."

SAMUEL JOHNSON
(English literary figure, perhaps the most quoted English writer after Shakespeare)

Let me share a personal story showing you how to regain lost confidence.

One morning, while on a weekly teleconference at work, something happened. I had been doing well with facing my fears and hadn't had a real panic attack in months. As I looked over the meeting agenda, I realized that I was going to have to give an oral status report. I became worried. I put myself into a negative and very anxious state and was inching toward a panic attack as my turn drew close.

By the time my name was called, I had become so anxious that I actually stood up at my desk. I had to stretch and flex my muscles to release this extra energy and calm myself down. Then, to my surprise, just five seconds after I began speaking I was fine.

Afterward, I worried about the events of that morning. I had worked hard to make progress with my anxiety, but the negative thoughts of hopelessness were starting to reappear. To regain my confidence, I picked one of the hardest things I could think of doing at that stage of my recovery. I decided to take a crowded and slow el train home that evening.

I was a wreck waiting for the train, but I was determined. As usual, after a few minutes in this packed train, I was calm and collected. I did it! The positive feelings I had then washed away the negative thoughts that had filled my mind since the teleconference that morning. I got an instant boost of much-needed self-confidence.

"If I can't, I must."

TONY ROBBINS
(self-help guru famous for working with world leaders, celebrities, and high-profile athletes)

Think about that for a minute. When you do something you thought you couldn't do, you open new doors. You've disproved the law of the universe, or at least your universe. It makes you wonder, "Hmm. . . What other doubts I have about myself are false?" Then. . . magic happens.

At work the next day, I had to deal with another teleconference. This time, however, I didn't become nearly as anxious. Facing the el had raised my confidence, and I could face this fear more easily.

When you face any fear, other fears diminish. Believe me, when you begin to overcome Fear A, Fears B through Z are much less daunting. Once you get the confidence momentum started, it's hard to stop!

Join a group

When it comes to treating anxiety, I don't advocate traditional therapy. I don't believe lying on a couch and complaining that your mom loved your sister more does much for solving your anxiety problems of today. However, I do recommend seeking out a center that specializes in treating anxiety.

When I joined a group at an anxiety treatment center, tremendous relief washed over me. I discovered that many other "normal" people were going through the exact same experiences with anxiety. They gathered from all walks of life, men, women, white collar, blue collar, students, and retirees. It was good to know I wasn't alone in this.

Hearing others in the group tell about their own bouts with anxiety and panic attacks made me feel connected to them. Any barriers that existed on the surface evaporated.

I had a good experience and highly recommend joining a support group. Most medium-sized cities will likely have a center specializing in treating anxiety. Check the phone book or turn to the Internet to locate such centers.

You may also access our online community where anyone and everyone is welcome to discuss all aspects of anxiety. Everything is completely free and anonymous and can be accessed here: http://www.alifelessanxious.com/forum

Head down the mountain

Snowboarding is a useful analogy for facing your fear. When you first stand up on a snowboard, you may feel as if you have no control or balance. Because you feel you are not in control, you precariously advance sideways down the mountain, falling often, afraid of gathering too much speed.

However, when you point the nose of your snowboard directly down the mountain and into the danger and your greatest fear, you begin to take control. The faster you travel, the more control over your snowboard you have and the less effort it takes to steer. In other words, the faster you move toward your fear, the more control you gain.

Naturally, you crash sometimes. Catching the edge of a snowboard in the snow will always result in a hard crash. The first time this happens, it can shake you up; you may tend to ride less aggressively. Although, you may be skilled and experienced, the fresh memory of that last crash and the fear of another may change your approach.

This is just like working through your exposure hierarchy. You make good progress until one negative experience makes you question the whole exposure process. Don't let this happen!

Recognize this for what it is—just a little bump in the road. Don't turn a speed bump into a mountain. This is where your determination and quest for freedom from your fears must kick in and help push you to continue.

When you do encounter a setback, just try your best to keep things in perspective. Realize that it's only temporary. You aren't completely derailed and powerless. Get back on that snowboard, and keep making your way down the mountain.

Benefits of reflection and facing your fears

"Everything negative that happens to you is a hidden opportunity. And the seeds for all solutions, for all problems are in the problem itself. The cure is in the illness."

WAYNE DYER
(author of more than 30 self-help and inspirational books)

The benefits of my entire experience have been incredibly far reaching. Facing my problems and learning to overcome them has touched every aspect of my life. The inspired feelings and thoughts I now have had always been there, it just took facing my fears and exploring who I am to reveal them.

Enduring my struggles with anxiety and panic has humanized me. Having felt vulnerable myself, I have developed empathy for others who have suffered through other dreadful things. I've been lucky not to be afflicted by major physical health problems, so I had no frame of reference when it came to deep suffering. That changed when I became a prisoner of anxiety.

If it hadn't been for panic and anxiety, I would not have explored myself so deeply. I would probably not have read the books whose passages have forever changed my life. I would not have been able to help others who have and are suffering through similar problems. When I hear people describe the problems in their lives, I empathize with their tears and sadness and frustration. I know that I have grown emotionally, and I am very thankful.

As you begin to make progress in overcoming your anxiety and reclaiming your life, you will grow in ways you never imagined. Each day will be filled with opportunity and promise. We're going to get you there!

COPING SKILLS:
HOW TO CALM YOURSELF

You may be very anxious when you begin facing your fears, even if you start by addressing minor ones. To help you, here are some coping skills you can learn to help calm yourself down in the heat of the moment. I've tried many techniques and want to share those that I've found most helpful.

By the way—just checking—you did follow the instructions from the previous chapter and can reference your anxiety hierarchy, right? If you haven't, go back and do this right now.

Mental coping skills

In dealing with exposures, remember this: Your physical symptoms related to panic and anxiety result from your negative and fearful thoughts. You decide what you want to focus on.

Naturally, when you begin the process of putting yourself through increasingly difficult exposures, you are going to feel anxious. But this is good! Part of fixing your flawed thinking is to face these seemingly threatening situations. When you come out unharmed, you will realize that your worry and anxiety were a waste of time and energy. Let's get started and learn some effective mental coping skills.

Before the exposure, put yourself in a positive state
I suspect that you spend much of your time worrying about what-if situations and avoiding them. That means you are often in a non-resourceful and fearful state. You don't feel strong or confident, and the last action you want to take is facing whatever you're afraid of. Believe me, I know the feeling.

To become more positive and resourceful, here's what you can do.

Mood-changing music
Have you ever attended a group exercise class at a gym or fitness center? Such classes provide an energetic and motivating environment to help you get the best workout possible. What's their secret? They blast high-energy music with thumping beats to get you up and moving and giving it your all. When it's time to cool down, slow and soothing music is played, and your pace and mindset follow suit.

Music is powerful. Harness this power by listening to the right types of music. Sure, sometimes it feels good to sing the blues, but that doesn't do much to inspire or energize you. Organize an inspirational playlist on your iPod or create a tape or CD and bring it with you. Starting your day off listening to such music will help you get into the most resourceful and optimistic mood.

Not only do I listen to mood-altering music before facing an exposure, I also often listen to it during the first part of the exposure. For example, when I was re-acclimating myself to riding the el in Chicago, I would listen to upbeat music on my iPod during the ride itself. I viewed it as a kind of security blanket. The music helped distract me.

Later, as you progress, you can wean yourself off of such aids so you fully experience your exposures.

Feel triumphant

Instead of dwelling on how difficult it will be to endure an upcoming situation, think about how great you'll feel once it's over. See yourself walking away with your arms raised in triumph.

Inspire yourself

Sometimes you need to be inspired. Read inspirational quotes, books, or religious texts and stories before and during an exposure. For example, I've often taken an inspirational book of quotes with me on many crowded buses, trains and planes. Reading them is much more relaxing than studying the in-flight emergency exit procedures!

Find the humor

"Laughter is time spent with the gods."

JAPANESE PROVERB

This saying was displayed on a magnet on our refrigerator by my mother when I was growing up. As long as I live, I will never forget it. I believe it's true. I don't think anything puts a person in a better state of mind than genuine laughter. The more you can laugh at what happens to you, the better off you'll be. I sometimes read a funny quote or listen to a stand-up comedian on my iPod before and/or during the exposure.

Treating myself every morning by reading my favorite comic strip has proved fun, too. No matter what activities my day may bring, laughing every morning helps me keep my perspective.

"Laughter is an instant vacation."

MILTON BERLE
(Hollywood icon known for his sense of humor)

Look around you. Find the humor in what you see. Here's how I do this. If I am in a crowded bus and see two people sitting next to each other who appear completely different, I imagine what their mental dialogues might be. How can you not laugh when you imagine what the nun sitting next to the kid with the green mohawk and nose ring is thinking?

Regardless of where you are, when you take a good look around you, will never run out of things to laugh at.

Picture yourself *completely freaking out!*

> *"Laugh at yourself first, before anyone else can."*
>
> ELSA MAXWELL
> (American gossip columnist and professional hostess credited with creating the
> scavenger hunt for use in modern-day parties)

Focus on the ridiculousness of many of your thoughts. Used well, this can be a very important healing technique. Here's how.

If I was in a bus packed shoulder to shoulder with sixty people, my initial fears would be about freaking out, scrambling to escape that scene, and the embarrassment I would feel. But I found it amusing to picture myself *really* overreacting.
I would tell myself, "Okay, so you're afraid of freaking out a little bit? Well, how about picturing freaking out a lot? What if I took off my shirt and waved it over my head while screaming some Twisted Sister lyrics?"

Or if I was nervous in a big meeting awaiting my turn to speak, I'd ask myself, "What if I broke out into a freestyle rap song complete with b-box sound effects and started break dancing right here? What if, in the middle of a presentation, I jumped on the table and began riding an invisible pony around?"

As long as it makes you laugh, it works. Picture it!

Smile!
When that moment of truth arrives, and you've committed yourself to facing one of your fears, smile! Have you ever heard the saying, "Act as if"?

Smiling, even if it is somewhat forced, activates powerful positive forces and feelings. When it's time for you to give an important presentation or your plane takes off, force yourself to smile ear to ear as big as you can. Smiling and being upset at the same time is a hard thing to do.

Picture a wonderful and inspiring memory
Sometimes we forget just how far we've come and what we've accomplished. Reflect on some of the shining moments in your life. The day you hit the home run to win the game, the first time you learned to ride a bicycle without training wheels, your first kiss, graduation from high school or college. I know you have these strong, positive memories that make you feel good or proud. Close your eyes and remember those times. Remember the complete experiences and minute details. The related positive emotions will be that much more intense and moving.

For instance, I remember how proud I felt the day I walked across the stage and received my college degree. Hearing my family cheer for me as my name was announced thrilled me. I remember the excitement and sense of adventure I felt when I lived in Europe. I enjoyed so many wonderful experiences—the first time I gazed at the Alps, the smell of fresh bread in France, staring up at the ceiling of the Sistine Chapel. Recalling these memories puts me in a resourceful state of joy and pride, regardless of my situation. If you call up your own special memories, those wonderful feelings will come to you, and anxiety will fall away.

Turn it over to faith
Taking time each day to say prayers or think about an all-seeing, all-knowing power in control of the universe may comfort you. I'm

not trying to push my personal beliefs on you. Rather, I am sharing what helps me.

If I become anxious while stuck in a tough spot, I try to remember that some greater power has put me in this particular situation. I believe that I am *supposed* to be there. Then my thinking often shifts to: **What am I supposed to be learning from this experience? What specifically am I supposed to take away from it to better my life?**

I feel stronger because I believe I am there for a reason, and it is up to me to gain the most I can from the experience.

> *"If you knew who walked beside you at all times on this path that you have chosen, you would never experience fear or doubt again."*
>
> UNKNOWN AUTHOR from *A Course in Miracles*, a widely followed best-selling book that has spawned related works and study groups dedicated to learning from this huge (1,333 pages!) text

Just reading that quote makes me feel better immediately.

Famous motivational author and speaker Norman Vincent Peale offers the following mantra in his landmark book *The Power of Positive Thinking*:

> *"God is with me, God is helping me, God is guiding me."*
>
> NORMAN VINCENT PEALE

I've found that repeating this phrase to myself while stuck in a difficult spot can provide tremendous relief.

Will this matter a year from now?

If you think of the daily happenings of your life on a larger scale, you'll realize how small in the grand scheme of the universe a crowded elevator ride or speaking at a meeting really is.

Think about your life as a whole. Imagine looking back at it from your deathbed. If you were old and dying and reviewing your life's events, would this stupid bus ride or public-speaking event cross your mind? Would you even be able to recall it?

Probably not. So why should you give this tiny piece of your existence so much power and attention?

Dare yourself

Another way I've found to deal with scary what-if thoughts is to challenge yourself to act them out. If you are in a meeting at work and your scary thoughts are centered on yelling out something highly inappropriate, dare yourself to do it. Tell yourself, "Okay, buddy, you want to yell something out, then do it! Do it now!" You may be surprised when nothing happens.

The thought simply goes away. I'm telling you, this works!

Think of this like getting pushed around by a bully on the playground. The bully, loud and intimidating, loves to use fear as his primary weapon. But eventually, one day, he has pushed you too far. His constant torment has finally triggered your need for self-preservation and right to happiness, and you fight back. You find out the bully was never as tough as you (or even he) thought he was, and he doesn't bother you again.

Make your own Valium

Before you grab your chemistry set, let me explain. Valium is a prescription drug that has a tranquilizing and calming effect. It is often used to treat symptoms of extreme anxiety.

Dr. Wayne Dyer shared a funny story during one of his talks about the famous inspirational figure Deepak Chopra. On a long overseas flight, Deepak was seated next to an American businessman who was ordering a cocktail every fifteen minutes. The man offered to buy Deepak a drink, to which he replied, "I'm making my own."

Just as we create anxious thoughts and feelings in our minds, we can also create calming and relaxing ones. When we put ourselves into a relaxed state, we experience the same soothing effects. Our body produces and releases its own calming chemicals in the brain. You don't need a pill to feel this way.

When you find yourself becoming anxious, visualize your mind producing these calming substances. Feel the warm and soothing effects as they spread throughout your entire body. As they pass through your chest, feel your heartbeat slow down. Feel them spread through your arms to the tips of your fingers, and through your legs to the tips of your toes. Your entire body becomes calm and still.

You can tap into these wonderful chemicals anytime you'd like. The more you practice this, the easier it becomes.

Just accept

This doesn't mean give up. Rather, just accept your situation. If you stop resisting and let go, you calm down almost immediately. When you are in the midst of panicking, you are struggling against the entire natural universe. Your negative thoughts are unnatural and clash with the natural flow of things. There may be greater forces at work. You are trying to control that which you cannot control, and the more you resist, the greater the struggle.

Instead of wasting your energy fighting your situation, allow it to happen and go with the flow.

Physical coping skills

I suspect many of you are still feeling so hopeless that you may not believe any of these mental coping techniques work. Take it from someone who once thought the same way—they absolutely do work! Physical tools can also help you gain confidence in facing your fears. Here's my proven-a-success list of breathing, muscle relaxation, and diversionary techniques.

Breathing techniques that work
Even if you don't meditate, something valuable you can take from the practice is being mindful of your breathing.

When you become anxious, your body responds by taking shallow, rapid breaths. You don't get enough oxygen into your blood with such abbreviated breaths, so your body hungers for more and intensifies the symptoms. This is the beginning of a panic attack for many, a form of hyperventilation. When you become scared by not being able to catch your breath, it can trigger a full-blown panic attack.

One technique that works well for me is this:

Inhale slowly and deeply through your mouth. Feel your chest fill and your diaphragm rise. Inhale until you can't possibly fit any more air into your lungs, and then hold it.

Pause for a full four or five seconds, and then slowly exhale through your nose.

Magic happens when you breathe this way. You activate your parasympathetic nervous system, which naturally acts to calm and relax you. Repeat this a few times, and you will find that you soon become relaxed and calm. When you master this technique, you'll find that it can result in an almost euphoric state of relaxation, which makes you feel completely at peace.

Get the muscles involved

For more help, add another technique. When you finish inhaling and begin holding your breath, try to tense every muscle in your body as hard as you can. Then hold each one in this tense state for at least five to ten seconds. After this, instantly relax every single muscle and almost go limp while slowly exhaling through your nose. You will feel the tension and scary anxious energy leave your body with your breath.

Rely on this technique. It really works!

Snap yourself out of it!

Once you have committed yourself to facing a fear, you may find negative and panicky thoughts immediately begin to swirl in your mind.

Try physically jolting yourself out of this state. I literally snap myself out of it by jolting my body in one powerful shake. Sometimes this takes the form of sharply turning my head in another direction and forcing my mind to stop focusing on negative thoughts. Other times, I make a fist as hard and fast as I can. If I'm anxious on a plane, I sometimes get up out of my seat and go to the bathroom and splash some cold water on my face. Remember the classic comedy movie *Airplane*? One of the passengers becomes hysterical imagining that the plane is going to crash and is yelling and screaming uncontrollably. One by one the passengers go up to her and shake her. Some even slap her face to get her to stop. As the camera pans out, you see more than a dozen passengers (including a nun) lined up. All have punching gloves, and some have crowbars waiting for their turn.

When I'm anxious during a flight, I picture fellow passengers on the plane lining up to do the same to me, and I can't help but laugh! This instantly snaps me out of my anxious state.

Once you "peak," you gain immunity

Once you reach peak anxiety and experience extreme physical symptoms—meaning the worst possible panic attack levels—the feelings will quickly dissipate and you will soon be fine.

You will find as I have that your racing mind gives up and realizes there is no danger and that you do not need to panic. Understanding and believing this will help reduce your fear of panic attacks.

DITCH THE MEDICATION

When I first took prescription medication for my panic attacks (mind you, I still had no idea what was happening to me at the time), I saw little improvement in my anxiety. I tried a few different drugs and eventually settled on one that seemed to help. My symptoms improved, and I didn't have a panic attack for a few months. I thought my problems were solved. I was miserable from the numbing side affects, but I thought it was worth it.

—Yet, when I was facing my fear of public speaking, I still had a full-blown panic attack after having been on this medication for more than four months. What did that tell me? That medicine wasn't going to fix this. Something else was causing my problems.

I'm certainly not saying that I'm 100 percent against medication to help treat panic disorder and anxiety problems. I know it can provide some relief. Medication may make recovery easier. However, I am firm in my stance that you don't *need* medication to beat anxiety.

Some people insist that anxiety problems stem from a chemical imbalance in the brain. They feel the only way to remedy this is by taking antidepressants or anti-anxiety medication to rebalance the brain's chemistry.

Others offer the possibility that the reason the brain's chemistry is off is due to improper and maladaptive thinking. Thus, they conclude the brain can be put back into natural balance by learning how to think properly and positively. I am certainly of this opinion, and I use my own recovery as proof.

You see, the only time I saw any significant and lasting improvement in my condition was when I began to grasp how my negative and scary thoughts were affecting me. As I began to think properly, learned to meditate, and surrounded myself with positive and inspirational circumstances, my anxiety faded. This was without *any* medication.

It's like boiling pasta

Have you ever cooked pasta? Many chefs swear that adding salt to the water brings out more flavor in the pasta. But what happens when you pour salt into a boiling pot of water? Initially, the water stops boiling as the salt rapidly dissolves. After a few moments, the water boils again just as furiously as before.

This is what happened to me while I was on anti-anxiety medication. I was simply adding salt to my boiling pot of anxiety and worry. I didn't do anything to turn down the heat, as I still had a mind full of unhealthy thoughts. Eventually my anxiety overpowered any calming effects of the medication. Once again, I had a boiling pot of anxiety.

You have to fix what's causing your problems instead of only treating the symptoms. When you have successfully done this, you will see that you don't need the medication.

I know how hard it is when you first have panic attacks. I would have injected heroin into my eyeballs if I thought it would make the attacks go away. You may want to take prescription medication at first. Just recognize that it's not a long-term solution.

If you properly employ the tactics I've laid out in Part II of this book, you too can achieve freedom from anxiety without depending upon medication.

INSPIRATION

Inspiration can come in many forms. Some people may become inspired by listening to a particular song, watching a powerful scene in a movie, or from reading an inspirational quote from an accomplished leader. Regardless of the source, finding inspiration is vital in overcoming your fears and getting your life back. Becoming emotionally motivated and creating a sense of urgency are vital. Go see speakers, movies, performers; anything that causes you to feel such moving emotions.

Ancient inspiration

> *"When the student is ready, the master will appear."*
>
> ZEN PROVERB

In reading and listening to various self-help programs, I've discovered that the same principles can be traced back thousands of years to Buddhism. Buddhism teaches us to be very observant of our thoughts, for they create our world. Wayne Dyer, Tony Robbins, and countless other self-help teachers preach this same concept. We create our own world with our thoughts. We can make them wonderful or horrifying. The choice is ours.

When I was an overworked consultant traveling in Germany, I was desperately seeking relief from my anxiety. One afternoon, before flying there for a one-month business trip, I popped into a bookstore and bought a few books on Eastern philosophies and Buddhism. I was hopeful that I would get something useful from them. Maybe they would inspire me in some way. Little did I know that I had happened upon a few gems.

One book was *Voices of Insight* by Sharon Salzberg. This work includes accounts of Westerners who have spent many years in the Far East learning from and practicing Buddhism with masters such as Ajahn Chah, a Buddhist monk. Her book is filled with many of his teachings, and I want to share this one as told by Jack Kornfield, who was a student of Ajahn Chah. Please note in the following passage that *dharma* can be viewed as the "path of awakening" in the Buddhist world.

> "*Ajahn Chah described two levels of spiritual practice. On the first level, you use Dharma to become comfortable. You become virtuous and a little kinder. You sit and quiet your mind, and you help make a harmonious community. There are genuine blessings of this comfortable level of Dharma. But the second kind of Dharma, he said, is to discover real freedom of mind, heart, and spirit. This level of practice has nothing whatsoever to do with comfort. Here you take every circumstance of life and work with it to learn to be free.*
>
> "*Ajahn Chah spoke of the second kind of Dharma the day I arrived at his monastery. He smiled and welcomed me by saying, 'I hope you're not afraid of suffering.' I was shocked. 'What do you mean? I came here to practice meditation, to find inner peace and happiness.' He explained, 'There are two kinds of suffering. The first is the suffering that causes*

more suffering, that we repeat over and over. The second is the suffering that comes when we stop running. The second kind of suffering can lead you to freedom."'

What really hits home with me are the final three sentences, pointing out the patterns that we tend to repeat. We continue to suffer and live a life in which we are walking on eggshells, constantly avoiding that which frightens us. But in the end, this great teacher offers exploring the possibility of no longer running—instead, confronting your fears.

In *Voices of Insight*, Joseph Goldstein, author and cofounder of the Insight Meditation Society in Barre, Massachusetts, reinforces the importance of finding courage to face our fears.

"At this stage of our journey, the Great Struggle, the question for us is whether we can generate this courage, this courageous heart, not from some external model of how we should be, but from within ourselves—from our own interest, our own willingness, our own passion for freedom. It is this courage that allows us to keep playing at the edge of exploration, the edge of discovery, even when it's uncomfortable, when we don't want to be there. When we're at the edge of what is known, new possibilities emerge."

This passage inspires me to keep pushing myself past my comfort zone and into the unknown. To achieve freedom, you have to put yourself in difficult situations and remain there, no matter how hard it is for you.

While suffering from panic, I couldn't imagine being in difficult situations I feared because I *thought* I knew how I would react. However, as this passage instructs, when you take fate into your own hands and put yourself on the line, new possibilities come to light. The past is the past.

Another book that has had a dramatic effect on my life is *The Art of Happiness* by the Dalai Lama and Howard C. Cutler, M.D.

Dr. Cutler is an American psychiatrist who spent many hours interviewing the Dalai Lama to gain an understanding of how Buddhist principles may be applied to the lives of Westerners. The Dalai Lama is the spiritual leader of the Tibetan Buddhists. He is recognized as a symbol of peace, love, and understanding, and serves as a source of inspiration to millions worldwide.

In the book, following along the subject of suffering and facing your fears, the Dalai Lama offers this bit of wisdom:

> *"Trying to avoid our problems or simply not thinking about them may provide temporary relief, but I think that there is a better approach. If you directly confront your suffering, you will be in a better position to appreciate the depth and nature of the problem. If you are in a battle, as long as you remain ignorant of the status and combat capability of your enemy, you will be totally unprepared and paralyzed by fear. However, if you know the fighting capability of your opponents, what sort of weapons they have and so on, then you're in a much better position when you engage in the war. In the same way, if you confront your problems rather than avoid them, you will be in a better position to deal with them."*

When you educate yourself about anxiety (which you are doing by reading this book!), you take away much of its power. Learning about something in great detail that you fear makes it less daunting and more familiar. And just like Ajahn Chah, the Dalai Lama insists that the best solution to overcome any fear is to confront it.

> *"In order to achieve happiness, you need a variety of approaches and methods to deal with and overcome the varied and complex negative mental states. And if you are seeking to overcome certain negative ways of thinking, it is not possible to accomplish that simply by adopting a particular thought or practicing a technique once or twice. Change takes time."*

Change is hard. It sometimes seems we are programmed to resist change. I know I certainly have comfort zones and a routine that I am very comfortable with. Any time I am pushed beyond this comfort zone, it is difficult. People become set in their ways, and it feels unnatural to change a behavior that has become habit.

You have to be dedicated and really work at changing. After all, your thoughts didn't become so extremely harmful and irrational overnight, so naturally it's going to take some time to turn them around. Try not to become frustrated as you slowly make progress.

"Don't ever give up!"

If you want to be inspired, watch the video clip of Jim Valvano's speech given at the 1993 ESPY Awards (awards created by ESPN sports network). Mr. Valvano was a very colorful and outgoing college basketball coach who had terminal cancer with no idea how much longer he'd live at the time of this speech.

His speech is simply one of the most touching and inspirational things I have ever heard. At some of my lowest moments, I've watched the clip of his speech on the Internet. It never fails to move me and fill me with hope and inspiration. The speech may be viewed at the official Web site: http://www.jimmyv.org.

The most memorable thing that people take from Mr. Valvano's speech is what became the catch phrase of the V Foundation for Cancer Research. In the end, he begs of us all, "Don't give up. Don't ever give up!" So don't!

Inspiration from television and movies

Take notice of what you're watching on television. While they may receive colossal ratings, graphic shows about grisly crime scenes and murder investigations don't quite leave you with a warm and fuzzy feeling. Following suit, the nightly news programs know what sells and are often filled with shocking stories of violence and bloodshed. These are not images you want dancing around your head when you're trying to create a more optimistic outlook on life.

Instead, opt for more positive and lighthearted options. Any show or movie that you find funny is always a good choice. When you're laughing, you are truly feeling the bliss of life. Any programs that show ordinary people doing extraordinary things are wonderful as well. We all need heroes!

THE CLOCK IS TICKING

Create a sense of urgency. Now! Every day you've lived with your anxiety and allowed it to control your life is a day you haven't truly lived. Many of us tell ourselves that we'll eventually face our problems when we're feeling stronger. I've learned that it's actually facing them that makes you stronger, not *planning* to face them.

"An ounce of action is worth a ton of theory."

FRIEDRICH ENGELS
(German social scientist and philosopher who developed communist theory along with Karl Marx)

Think about this: Do you want to look back at your life and know you spent most of it worrying about your fears, or do you want to look back and know that you lived the way you wanted to live?

Seize this day. Start right now.

"Make each day your masterpiece."

JOHN WOODEN
(legendary basketball coach who guided his UCLA men's team to an astonishing 10 national championships in 12 years)

PART III

APPLYING THE LESSONS

APPLYING THE LESSONS

I USED PART II OF THIS BOOK to provide you with information, background, and tools to help empower you to overcome your fears and anxieties.

In Part III, I'd like to conclude this book by sharing with you exactly how I used these tools to empower myself.

I hope my story gives you the courage and inspiration to keep striving to conquer anxiety and panic. My life was miserable, and I was able to turn things around. I'm telling you from the bottom of my heart that, no matter how bad off and hopeless you think you are, there is hope for you!

I try, try again

If you recall, at the end of Part I, I hit rock bottom. This was absolutely the worst period of my life. I had been struggling with panic attacks off and on for five years. Twice I thought I had overcome them, only to relapse on both occasions. But this time, I was determined to permanently overcome my problems. I wanted to build a solid foundation for the rest of my life, one that would make another relapse unlikely.

My first major challenge was my inevitable return to flying. Remember that I had a panic attack on a plane while flying to my friend's wedding in New York City, an event that caused me a tremendous amount of anticipatory anxiety. My already booked flight home for Thanksgiving was my first major challenge.

I was flying out on a Wednesday night after work, which meant that I would have to endure riding the crowded el to the airport during rush hour. Since my friend's wedding, I had begun re-acclimating myself to the el by riding it during uncrowded lunch hours. However, I was still dreadfully anxious about riding it during crowded rush hours.

Whatever I could do in advance to avoid having a panic attack on the el or the flight, I did it.

During my lunch hour at work, I went into overdrive at the gym. I'm sure everyone there thought I was either crazy or on cocaine. I sprinted on the treadmill and lifted weights as intensely as my out-of-shape body allowed. I tried to drain my body of all excess energy to make it very difficult to become anxious. I returned to work afterward and felt remarkably better and more relaxed in the afternoon. Thank you, post-workout endorphins!

I made the time to exercise, for I knew it would help me.

As my workday wound down, it was time to head to the airport. In downtown Chicago, it makes no sense to take a taxi to either airport as the el is so much cheaper and takes you directly there. Besides, I was flying at 7:00 p.m., and the road traffic would have taken hours. Also, part of me wanted to rise to the challenge of riding the el.

I hadn't ridden the el regularly during rush hour in more than six months. But thinking about my upcoming flight (which scared me even more than the el), something occurred to me.

I knew the el would freak me out. But at some point, logic kicked in and I thought to myself, "Okay, I'm about to get on a plane and fly for two hours, and I'll just have to get through it. That isn't much different than riding the el for half that time. Hell, the el should be easier and a good way to prepare for the flight!"

So, I dragged my luggage down to the Clinton Blue Line el stop. I walked to the end of the el platform with the aim of riding in the last car, which usually has the fewest passengers. As the train pulled up, every single car, including the last one, was nearly full. I told myself I wasn't going to run, and I didn't. With my large, awkward rolling luggage, I worked my way into the crowded car and into one of the corners. The loudspeaker sang its familiar tune, "*Ding dong*, doors closing," and off we went.

I swallowed hard several times and employed many breathing techniques, I can tell you that! At the second stop, the train became completely packed. Considering I had my large rolling luggage and was wearing a backpack, I was literally stuck, crammed into a corner of the train car. Even if I had desperately wanted to get out, it would have been nearly impossible to escape before the doors closed again. I was stuck, and my head was starting to fill with negative thoughts, but I fought them off.

As the Blue Line snaked its way through downtown and picked up even more passengers, I was slowly calming down. Just a few minutes into this crowded train ride, I was fine. Actually, I was better than fine, I was thrilled!

I stood my ground, and the panic and anxiety symptoms went away. Before I knew it, most passengers had come and gone, and we were heading toward O'Hare. I grabbed a seat and enjoyed the rest of the ride.

I still had the flight ahead of me. I distinctly remember telling myself, "Well, that wasn't really a victory, for it wasn't a true test. The flight will be much harder. You'll definitely freak out on the flight; the el was nothing."

Why did I do this to myself?

I'm not really sure, but I think we become so conditioned to telling ourselves that we can't do something that when we try to praise ourselves and be positive, it feels foreign and incorrect. It's like an exercise you would find in a child's workbook—circle the one that doesn't belong! You somehow choose to ignore the positive feelings and thoughts you are having and revert back to the negative ones you're used to having.

You have to unlearn what you've been conditioning your brain to think and feel.

At the airport, having just completed a challenging train ride, I had ninety minutes to wait before my flight. I stewed about in the airport, flipping through some inspirational books and reading my favorite quotes. The flight was delayed twice, which gave me even more time to become anxious.

Finally, they called us to board. Surprisingly, the plane was one of those tiny little puddle-jumpers. With only twenty rows and a low ceiling, this was far from ideal. Just ducking my head to get through the door and into the tiny plane triggered my claustrophobia.

I was lucky. I sat next to a very nice talkative woman who was returning home to Oklahoma for the holiday. We talked and shared our holiday plans. Our conversation before takeoff helped calm me.

As the tiny plane lifted off the ground, my heart was pounding. I was practicing my breathing and relaxation techniques, and that was all I could do. I was stuck on this plane for two hours, so I had to find a way to get through it!

Then something happened. Since much younger days, I have been fascinated by flying. Every flight I have ever taken, I would stare out the window for as long as I could, until the clouds blocked my view. The beauty and serenity I would feel looking down on the world from such a unique vantage point bewildered me.

While anticipating this flight, one of the most terrifying visualizations I imagined was looking out the window. I would then realize how high we were, and that I was stuck. But as the plane rose over the glimmering lights of Chicago, I did something I didn't think I would do. I leaned over and stared out the window just as I had when I was a child.

Just a few minutes into the flight, I was fine. I knew having a panic attack was practically impossible. I felt at peace. I distinctly remember walking to the back of the plane and using the tiny phone-booth-sized bathroom. I looked into the mirror, splashed some cold water on my face, and smiled my ass off. I clenched my fist in victory.

Near the end of the flight, I took a good look around at each person on the flight. It became clear to me that everyone in that plane was a person just like me. Worrying about embarrassing myself in front of them by having a panic attack didn't seem to matter. When you are in the midst of facing your greatest fears, you just might have your most powerful insights.

Later, we landed and I claimed my sweet reward: seeing my family for the first time in months and being home for Thanksgiving for the first time in six years. Now, I can't guarantee that when you face your worst fears, you will be rewarded with home cooking like my mom's,* but you will be rewarded with the inexplicably energizing and inspiring feeling that only comes when you run directly at your fear.

*Disclaimer: You'll actually never get home cooking as good as my mom's unless we invite you over, for she is the greatest cook on earth.

EPIPHANIES

What I've learned during the past five years of reading books, reflecting on my life, and facing down my fears is: the more you let your inner child out to play, the happier you'll be.

Do you remember what it was like to be a child? Everything was brand new, mysterious, and exciting. Little was tainted by bad experiences yet, and you didn't worry about what other people thought of you if you tried something. You just did it if you wanted to do it. That was all.

"It is the childlike mind that finds the kingdom."

CHARLES FILLMORE
(professor emeritus of linguistics and one of the founders of cognitive linguistics)

I encourage you to let your inner child out to play. Explore and learn and ask questions. Then share and experience the joy and wonderment of it all.

Finding the combination

Do you know what an epiphany is? Think of it as a moment of revelation and insight. For me, it's a powerful instant where concepts I've been attempting to grasp come together and click—sort of like a combination lock when you dial in the correct sequence of numbers. Suddenly, it all makes sense. In dealing with anxiety, I have experienced this a few times.

One spring, I had a click moment. This time, it was during another true test on the 134 Stockton Express Bus.

I had had a good day at work, very busy, but didn't get to speak at our weekly meeting as I had anticipated. Not feeling like I was tested at all that day, I was hungry to push myself. I wanted to do something big and pick a fight with my fears. I had taken the 134 a number of times but only once when it was really packed. Even then, it was very early in the morning, and I knew that the express part of the ride on Lake Shore Drive would last only five to ten minutes due to traffic. When we're moving fast, it makes the ride louder and more distracting and makes me feel as if we're getting to safety faster.

Traveling on Lake Shore Drive after work, however, is a completely different story. Stop-and-go traffic is normal then, and I knew it would be a great challenge for me. Letting a few non-express buses go by, I felt confident knowing I was going out of my way to once again pick a fight with my fears. As I boarded the bus, I headed for the back corner, which becomes the most cramped and trapped part of the bus. It was a true test.

Long before we reached the last stop before traveling express on Lake Shore Drive, the bus was jam-packed with every seat taken and at least forty people standing in every available space in the aisle.

As the bus made its way toward Lake Shore Drive, I saw that it was bumper-to-bumper traffic in all four northbound lanes. Perfect! As we finally made it to the onramp, I could see nothing but stop-and-go traffic.

Yet as I sat there in the back of this crowded bus, I looked around and smiled to myself. I knew I couldn't have a panic attack. I had worked hard at facing my fears and correcting my faulty thinking, therein finding the right combination to unlock my anxiety problems. Click!

That bus ride home was the best one of my life.

> *"What's neat about human beings? When they put themselves on the line, they come through. They discover they're much more than they think they are when they have to perform."*
>
> TONY ROBBINS, from his best-selling book *Unlimited Power* (popular author and speaker in the field of personal development)

Facing public speaking

I knew one of the key ingredients in my recovery would be Toastmasters. The previous summer, I had joined Extreme Toastmasters, a highly motivated club, in a last ditch effort to become more comfortable in front of a crowd before my buddy's wedding. However, after the wedding, I stopped attending meetings.

Now I was ready. I vowed that I would start attending the meetings regularly. No matter how hard it got, I would keep going.

> *"And the day came when the risk to remain tight in a bud became more painful than the risk it took to blossom."*
>
> ANAÏS NIN
> (diarist and author of French surrealistic-styled avant-garde novels)

After six months off, I returned to the weekly meetings. By just showing up and sitting in that seat, I had already won a huge victory. While all my thoughts kept telling me to avoid this situation, that I didn't have to be there, that this was going to be insanely difficult, I didn't listen to them. I went anyway, despite what my body, and most of my mind, was telling me to do.

Just as I structured a plan to slowly face increasingly difficult situations on public transportation, I did the same to overcome my fear of public speaking.

The beauty of Toastmasters is that you can do whatever you like at whatever pace you like. For the first few meetings, I made the required introduction and answered an improvisational opening question. I had countless opportunities to give a prepared speech or assume a meeting role, but I didn't.

Happy Valentine's Day to me! The holiday happened to fall on a Wednesday, the day our Toastmasters group meets. With a heavy snowfall (imagine that, during February in Chicago!) and the holiday, the group was small, maybe ten people instead of the usual twenty-plus. This made me somewhat less nervous, but I was still a ball of anxiety.

With so few people, everyone had to actively participate in the meeting. I realized I would be highly encouraged to give an improvisational speech for two to three minutes. When it came time to assign the timekeeper's role, the president, Tim, volunteered me. Although this made me very nervous, I smiled and accepted. After all, I was there to push myself.

They also needed someone to give an evaluation of one of the speakers. Again Tim turned to me and said, "I think you should do that, too." Now I was really smiling, knowing he was right. This was exactly what I needed, to leave the kiddy pool and jump into the deep end.

I did great! Way better than I ever imagined I could. I even became comfortable enough by the end of that meeting that my true personality came out. I added my own brand of humor to my speaking that night and felt a deep sense of accomplishment and pride.

Tim pushed me along faster than I would have gone at my own pace. For this, I thank him. This reminds me of a great quote.

"'Come to the edge,' he said. They said, 'We are afraid.'
'Come to the edge,' he said. They came. He pushed them
. . .and they flew."

GUILLAUME APOLLINAIRE
(French poet, writer, and art critic credited with coining the term *surrealism*)

Just remember: You don't need to have someone else push you;
you can always push yourself!

DOING THE IMPOSSIBLE

"You must do the things that you cannot do—you gain
strength, courage, and confidence by every experience
in which you really stop to look fear in the face."

ELEANOR ROOSEVELT
(former first lady of the U.S. and humanitarian who worked extensively for
human rights with the United Nations)

As I faced fear after fear, I began to grow. It felt wonderful. A
funny thing happened, too. After I had graduated from one level
of comfort and moved onto the next, it became more of a fun
challenge. My competitive spirit was awakened. I often viewed it as
me competing against my anxiety, and I wanted to win. Each time
I voluntarily faced my fears, I viewed it as if I was attacking the
enemy first and catching him off guard. Victory was mine!

Feeling good again

During my worst anxiety-filled days, I remember one morning, walking to work in downtown Chicago, I saw a gardener watering plants. I thought, "Want to switch jobs?" I had to attend a meeting later that day, and I would undoubtedly have to speak. I was a nervous wreck.

Many months later and in a much better state of mind, I passed the same gardener in the same spot. This time I thought how grateful I was to have my job. I also felt proud of how far I had come in overcoming my fear. Facing your fears can change your life in so many wonderful ways.

SUMMARY: WHAT WORKED

This is the part of the book where I tie it all together and list the points I really want to drive home. I've told you my personal story to break down the barriers and prove to you that you can overcome panic attacks and social anxiety.

I've given you some information on how anxiety works, what feeds it and what provides relief, and I handed you a roadmap that leads to personal freedom. Let's review the most important parts.

What Worked

1) **Systematically facing my fears**

2) **Not constantly focusing on my anxiety and things I dread**

3) **Being grateful for what I have and remembering it daily**

4) Focusing on my aspirations and what I want out of life daily

5) Using visualization in a positive way, imagining the most positive possible outcome in every situation

6) Focusing on staying in the present moment

7) Seeing the good in people and situations

8) Daily positive affirmations

9) Meditation and spending time every day alone with my thoughts

10) Loving myself unconditionally

Looking forward

What does the future hold for me? I will likely always have some anxiety in my life, but that doesn't have to be bad. Anxiety can help prepare you by forcing you to focus on a task and summon all of your skills. Healthy, nervous tension in moderate amounts makes us dig deep within ourselves to find our strengths and confidence and perform at our best. As long as you aren't living in constant fear and being debilitated by anxiety, you're fine.

> *"So, first of all, let me assert my firm belief that the only thing we have to fear is fear itself—nameless, unreasoning, unjustified terror which paralyzes needed efforts to convert retreat into advance."*
>
> FRANKLIN DELANO ROOSEVELT
> (the only U.S. president to serve more than two terms, he led the U.S. through the Great Depression of the 1930s)

It's okay to have fears; it's normal. After all, if our ancestors weren't afraid of man-eating dinosaurs, we probably wouldn't be here today! As long as you aren't deeply afraid of your own fear and you keep it in check, you will be fine. And once you learn this, understand this, believe this, and live this, you will be truly alive.

MASTERY OF FEAR

I remember watching a documentary featuring the comedian and actor Chris Rock. The cameras followed Chris around while he was promoting a comedy special he was to film for HBO.

One thing I distinctly remember was how nervous Chris said he was before he went onstage to perform. Talk about pressure! Here is this world-famous comedian being paid mega-bucks to perform onstage for an hour in front of an eager sold-out audience.

As a comedian and actor, Chris had performed hundreds or maybe even thousands of times. Yet he was still nervous and anxious before he took the stage. Of course, he was! This was a very high-pressure situation in which Chris absolutely had to perform. His career, reputation, and millions of dollars were at stake, so he'd better find a way to succeed and do well.

Backstage, you could see he was visibly nervous and trying to calm himself, but when it was show time, he confidently marched out on stage. As the audience quieted down, he started his act, and his show went flawlessly. He gave an amazing performance and never once missed a beat. What does this story tell you?

> *"Courage is resistance to fear, mastery of fear—not absence of fear."*
>
> MARK TWAIN
> (American humorist, satirist, and author of many famous works including
> *The Adventures of Huckleberry Finn*)

Chris looks at home on stage performing before a large crowd. Sure he gets nervous, but he doesn't let it stop him.

What can you take from this example? That it's okay to be nervous or anxious. Even when you conquer your panic attacks, you are still going to become somewhat anxious and nervous in similar situations. Do I still become anxious when boarding a crowded train or a plane? Sometimes. When it does happen, I know I'm going to be okay. I've already faced down such fears and know that they cannot get the best of me.

The same applies to new activities or situations that start to cause you some anxiety—for example, if you're on vacation and unexpectedly you have to take a ferry across a river. As you board, you realize you've never been on a ferry before and start to become anxious. Does this mean you're destined for a panic attack? No. You can handle it. Even if it's something for which you were unprepared, if the anxiety comes, you *know* you are still in control.

That's the beauty of facing your deepest and darkest fears. Once you know you can handle them, you can handle anything life throws at you. ANYTHING!

"Life is either a daring adventure, or nothing."

HELEN KELLER
(author, lecturer, and inspirational figure. She was the first deaf and blind person to graduate from college)

The future is yours

One of our presidents provided this bit of inspiration:

"It is not the critic who counts; not the man who points out how the strong man stumbled, or where the doer of deeds could have done them better. The credit belongs to the man who is actually in the arena, whose face is marred by dust and sweat and blood; who strives valiantly; who errs and comes short again and again; who knows the great enthusiasms, the great devotions; who spends himself in a worthy cause; who at the best, knows in the end the triumph of high achievement, and who, at the worst, if he fails, at least fails while daring greatly, so that his place shall never be with those timid souls who know neither victory or defeat."

THEODORE ROOSEVELT
(this American icon was the youngest-ever president of the U.S. at age 42)

I urge you to live your life as passionately and as fully as you possibly can. Don't let your fears stand in your way, for you are stronger than you can even imagine, and nothing can stop you from living the life that you deserve.

*"Not knowing when the dawn will come,
I open every door...."*

EMILY DICKINSON
(19th-century American poet)

Life is amazing, enjoy the journey!

APPENDIX A

ANXIETY HIERARCHY WORKSHEET

This worksheet will help you organize and rank the social situations that make you anxious, and form a plan of attack for facing and overcoming these fears.

Instructions

Filling out the sheet

List the different activities that make you anxious. Fill out as many activities as you feel necessary, starting with the most difficult.

Activity

Write down the specific activity that makes you anxious. Examples: Riding in a crowded elevator, talking to your boss, going to the dentist, etc.

Variables

Write down any variables that can occur during this activity that make it more difficult for you. Using the example of riding on a crowded train, variables may include the number of people in the train, duration of the journey, who you are with, etc.

Ranking

Assign each activity a ranking from 1–5, with 5 being the most difficult.

How to use this worksheet

Once you have completed filling out this worksheet, it's time to start facing your fears. You will start with the lowest ranking fears, and eventually work your way up to the most difficult. Your goal should be to work through one activity every two to four weeks and then graduate to the next most difficult activity.

Within each activity, use the variables you listed to increase the difficulty. For example, if riding in a crowded elevator is difficult for you, start out riding by yourself. Over the next two to four weeks, keep riding elevators that are more and more crowded. The goal in the end is to ride a jam-packed elevator. After you've done this at least a few times and become comfortable with it, you are ready to move on to the next activity in your hierarchy.

Tips for Getting the Most Out of This Worksheet

- Just because you've overcome some of the fears on your list, you shouldn't stop facing them. Repeatedly facing fears you have already overcome helps to maintain and even expand your self-confidence.

- Don't cheat by taking anti-anxiety medication, alcohol or other drugs when facing your fears. Your fear is self-created, and unless you put yourself through difficulty without the influence of foreign substances, you may not believe this.

Frequently Asked Questions

What if I have a fear of flying, going to a job interview, or another activity I can't face on a daily basis?

Some situations will be difficult to arrange. Plan to face such fears as soon as possible. In the meantime, it is helpful to create a comparable situation. For example, a commuter train that travels thirty minutes between stops would be good practice for a fear of flying. Or if you fear speaking at a staff meeting at work but don't have any scheduled for weeks, in the meantime you could face this fear by joining speaking clubs such as Toastmasters.

What if I have difficulty getting past a particular fear?

This is normal. To regain confidence, go back and face some of the other fears from your hierarchy that you've already overcome. This often provides the morale boost that you'll need to get past the next fear.

Example form:

Activity: *Riding a train*

Variables: *How crowded the train is, distance between stops, how fast the train travels, traveling with friends instead of alone, how far I have to take the train (number of stops), going through long tunnels, going over long bridges*

Difficulty Ranking 1–5: *5*

Activity: _____

_____

Variables: _____

_____

_____

_____

_____

_____

Difficulty Ranking 1–5: _____

◆ ◆

Activity: _____

_____

Variables: _____

_____

_____

_____

_____

_____

Difficulty Ranking 1–5: _____

Activity: _____

_____

Variables: _____

_____

_____

_____

_____

_____

_____

Difficulty Ranking 1–5: _____

✦ ✦

Activity: _____

_____

Variables: _____

_____

_____

_____

_____

_____

Difficulty Ranking 1–5: _____

Activity: _____

_____

Variables: _____

_____

_____

_____

_____

_____

_____

Difficulty Ranking 1–5: _____

◆ ◆

Activity: _____

_____

Variables: _____

_____

_____

_____

_____

_____

Difficulty Ranking 1–5: _____